Chinese Proverbs and Popular Sayings

With Observations on Culture and Language

Qin Xue Herzberg and Larry Herzberg

Stone Bridge Press • Berkeley, California

Published by
Stone Bridge Press
P.O. Box 8208
Berkeley, CA 94707
TEL 510-524-8732 • sbp@stonebridge.com • www.stonebridge.com

LIBRARY OF CONGRESS CATALOGING-IN-PUBLICATION DATA
Herzberg, Qin Xue.
  Chinese proverbs and popular sayings : with observations on culture and language / Qin Xue Herzberg, Larry Herzberg.
     p. cm.
  Text in Chinese and English.
  ISBN 978-1-933330-99-0
 1. Chinese language—Conversation and phrase books—English.
 2. Chinese language—Textbooks for foreign speakers—English.
 3. Language and culture—China. I. Herzberg, Larry. II. Title.
  PL1125.E6H523 2012
  495.1'83421--dc23
                              2011051251

Contents

Introduction

The proverbs of any country or culture contain the wisdom accumulated by its people over countless generations. China is the world's oldest continuous civilization, with over three thousand years of history. It is, therefore, hardly surprising that the Chinese language is a particularly rich source of wisdom. Arguably no other language or culture has such a treasure trove of proverbs and popular sayings that comment on every aspect of the human experience. It has as many as 20,000 literary idioms and tens of thousands of popular maxims and sayings, in addition to the pithy and profound quotes to be gleaned from three millennia of Chinese philosophy and literature.

Whenever people in the English-speaking world hear of an especially insightful or clever quote whose origin seems at first uncertain, we look first to the Bible and then to Shakespeare (and Mark Twain, if you're American). However, if the quote turns out to be from none of those major sources of wit and wisdom, we then assume it must be a Chinese saying—and very often that, indeed, proves to be the case. Every language and culture has many wonderful proverbs, of course, but no other matches Chinese in the sheer number of books and web sites devoted to it.

In Western countries like the United States, proverbs are heard less and less. Because individuality and creativity are prized, quoting age-old sayings is considered trite and outdated. Few young people in America today are heard to utter such maxims as "a stitch in time saves nine," "an ounce of prevention is worth a pound of cure," or "the early bird catches the worm." In China, however, sayings like the ones collected here are still peppered throughout daily speech. Their ancient culture gives the Chinese shared terms of reference in the thousands of phrases that sum up a situation in a few widely understood words. Employing the literary idioms demonstrates an educated background, and the use of the wide variety of sayings adds color and spice to conversation—to the point that the speech of someone who does not sprinkle his speech with these proverbs and maxims is said to have no flavor. In such a group-centered society, the emphasis is not on originality but, rather, on enjoying a shared cultural background. Wit and originality are displayed by cleverly changing the proverb's wording to say things in a fresh and humorous way.

The Chinese distinguish between literary idioms, which usually consist of four words and derive from ancient stories; five- and seven-word maxims, which are considered reasonably refined and often come in rhyming couplets; and popular sayings passed down by the "common people" over many generations, which typically have no set length or form. Because this book is intended for people in the West who might be unconcerned with these traditional categories but are only interested in pearls of wisdom from any source, we have mixed together all the various types of proverbs and sayings. We have also included a few of the most famous quotations from Chinese writers, poets, and philosophers in the past three thousand years. Of course, no book of pithy wisdom could do without a few choice phrases said to have been uttered by Confucius, the most revered of all Chinese sages.

The emphasis in this book, however, is on the popular sayings of the common people—which best represent the Chinese people as a whole.

In general, we have included only the most important and most beloved sayings known to most Chinese. Some books or web sites on Chinese sayings give too few, while others catalog far too many. We have tried here to strike a useful compromise between those two extremes, to reach what Confucius called the "Golden Mean."

This book is intended neither for scholars nor solely for those who already know Chinese. For those who are familiar with the language, we have included the original Chinese sayings in Chinese characters as well as in pinyin romanization. Our main goal, however, is to share with English speakers the rich variety of great insights and colorful metaphors that Chinese proverbs offer. This book is for all those who love pithy sayings about life, who love wordplay and clever turns of a phrase, and who want to gain a better understanding of Chinese culture.

What makes our book unique in the sea of other works available on this subject is that we attempt to show how Chinese proverbs and sayings reflect the Chinese view of the world. The book is divided into eighteen chapters, which group the sayings according to the various aspects of the human experience on which they comment, ranging from family and friends to money and morality to food. Each chapter begins with an explanation of the Chinese cultural background that relates to each of those topics.

Our fondest wish is that the reader will enjoy learning these nuggets of wisdom and witticisms and will be inspired to look deeper into Chinese history and culture. As you read the treasury of proverbs in the following pages, you will be struck by the similarity in joys and sorrows, problems and concerns, and virtues and vices experienced in both China and the West—a reflection of what the sage Confucius said nearly 2,500 years ago:

"Within the four seas, all men are brothers."
(All human beings in the world are one family.)
Sì hǎi zhī nèi jiē xiōngdì yě.
四海之内皆兄弟也。

1 Learning

Few other societies in the history of the world have for so long revered learning through study as have the Chinese. Starting as early as the seventh century, China chose all its government officials, except for the emperor, exclusively through an examination system based on the study of classical literature. Although it was much more difficult for a boy who did not come from the landed gentry to afford the books and instruction necessary to pass the various exams required to become a governor or imperial adviser, Chinese history is filled with examples of young men of humble beginnings who rose to prominent positions through self-education.

It is therefore only to be expected that Chinese culture has always promoted respect for teachers, because education has been the path to success. The most revered teacher of all time in China is, of course, Confucius. To this day temples all over the country are dedicated to his memory and to the realm of books and of study that he represents.

Here are some of the most famous quotes related to teaching, learning, and knowledge.

There is no end of books to read, just as there is no end of roads to travel

读不尽的书，走不完的路

TEACHERS

Whoever is your teacher, even for a day, consider your father (to respect and care for) your whole life.
Yírì wéi shī, zhōngshēn wéi fù.
一日为师，终身为父。—*Confucius*

When we walk together with three people, (at least) one of them will have something to teach us.
(Whenever you encounter any group of people, whether 3 or 33, there is something to be learned from at least one of them.)
Sān rén xíng, bì yǒu wú shī.
三人行，必有吾师。—*Confucius*

Never tire of studying, and never tire of teaching others.
Xué ér bú yàn, huì rén bú juàn.
学而不厌，诲人不倦。—*Confucius*

Every master has his/her own teaching methods; every trick has a different sleight of hand.
Gè shīfu gè chuánshòu, gè bǎxì gè biànshǒu.
各师傅各传授，各把戏各变手。

What you learn depends on whom you study with; if you study with a butcher, you'll never become a cobbler.

Gēn shénme rén xué shénme yàng, gēnzhe túfū xué bùchéng píjiàng.

跟什么人学什么样，跟着屠夫学不成皮匠。

If you study with a sorceress, you'll learn to dance about in a trance.

(The person with whom you study is the person you'll emulate.)

Gēnzhe shá rén xué shá rén, gēnzhe wūpó huì tiào shén.

跟着啥人学啥人，跟着巫婆会跳神。

To teach students for three years is to teach yourself.

(We learn something best by teaching it.)

Jiāoshū sānnián jiāo zìshēn.

教书三年教自身。

Give a man a fish, and he'll have food for a day [three meals]; teach a man to fish, and he'll have a skill to use all his life.

Shòu rén yǐ yú sān cān zhī xū, shòu rén yǐ yù zhōngshēn zhī yòng.

授人以鱼三餐之需，授人以渔终身之用。

First be a student, then be a teacher.

(One must learn something well before one can teach it to others.)

Xiān zuò xuéshēng, hòu zuò xiānsheng.

先做学生，后做先生。

Teaching by example is better than teaching by preaching.

(Actions speak louder than words; the best form of teaching is to model the virtues you teach.)

Shēn jiào zhòngyú yán jiào.

身教重于言教。

EXPERIENCE, INCLUDING FAILURE AND SUFFERING, CAN BE THE BEST TEACHER: THE SCHOOL OF HARD KNOCKS

If previous experiences are not forgotten, they can be the teachers in later matters.
(We can learn from previous experience only if we make the effort.)
Qián shì búwàng hòu shì zhī shī.
前事不忘后事之师。

Hearing about something a hundred times cannot compare to seeing it once for yourself.
("A picture is worth a thousand words"; "Seeing is believing")
Bǎi wén bùrú yíjiàn.
百闻不如一见。

If you do not experience anything, it's impossible to gain knowledge.
Bùjīng yí shì, bùzhǎng yí zhì.
不经一事，不长一智。

Eat/suffer a fall into the pit, gain in your wit.
(One often gains in wisdom after suffering [eating] misfortune.)
Chī yíqiàn zhǎng yízhì.
吃一堑长一智。

Without experiencing the cold of winter, one cannot appreciate the warmth of spring.
Bùjīng dōng hán, bùzhī chūn nuǎn.
不经冬寒，不知春暖。

Out of hunger comes wisdom; out of poverty comes cleverness.

Èchūlái de jiànshí; qióngchūlái de cōngming.

饿出来的见识；穷出来的聪明。

Receive one blow, and you'll learn a lesson; receive ten blows, and you'll end up a genius.

[lit.: you'll become like Zhuge Liang, a legendary master strategist and clever man]

Ái yì quán, dé yì zhāo, ái shí quán, biàn Zhūgé.

挨一拳，得一招；挨十拳，变诸葛。

Only if you have endured the bitterest suffering can you become a superior person.

Chī dé kǔ zhōng kǔ, fāng wéi rén shàng rén.

吃得苦中苦，方为人上人。

REGARDING TALENTED STUDENTS

[Expressing a teacher's hope that his student will surpass him in knowledge in the future]

Indigo comes from blue but exceeds blue [in its beauty].

Qīng chū yú lán, shèng yú lán.

青出于蓝，胜于蓝。

A fast horse needs only one lash of the whip; a quick student needs only one word [of wisdom].

Kuài mǎ yì biān, kuài rén yì yán.

快马一鞭，快人一言。

不经一事，不长一智

If you do not experience anything, it's impossible to gain knowledge

Teachers open the door; you enter by yourself.
[lit.: The master leads the student through the door, but perfecting one's skill is up to the student.]
(A teacher can only expose students to knowledge; then it's up to the student to work hard to learn what he or she has been taught.)
Shīfu lǐng jìn mén, xiūxíng zài gèrén.
师傅领进门，修行在个人。

If jade is not cut and polished, it can't be made into anything useful (and beautiful).
(You can't become anyone of consequence without the proper training and discipline.)
Yù bù zhuó bù chéng qì.
玉不琢不成器。

If you want people to know you, study diligently; if you are afraid for people to know you, don't do things that are wrong.
(To be known and respected, study hard; to remain unknown, do nothing bad.)
Yào rén zhī, zhòng qín xué; pà rén zhī, shì mò zuò.
要人知，重勤学；怕人知，事莫做。

LEARNING IS AN ENDLESS TASK THAT REQUIRES GREAT EFFORT

Live 'til you're old and study 'til you're old, but there's still 30% you'll never learn.
Huódào lǎo xuédào lǎo, hái yǒu sānfēn xuébudào.
活到老学到老，还有三分学不到。

You are never too old to learn.
Xué bú yàn lǎo.
学不厌老。

Even a hundred-foot-high bamboo can still grow taller.
[lit., advance one step further]
Bǎi chǐ gāntóu gèng jìn yíbù.
百尺竿头更进 步。

When trees get old, their trunks become half-empty [hollow]; when people get old, they are full of knowledge about many things.
Shù lǎo bàn xīn kōng; rén lǎo shìshì tōng.
树老半心空；人老事事通。

There is no end of books to read, [just as there is] no end of roads to travel.
(It is impossible for anyone to ever know all there is to know.)
Dú bú jìn de shū, zǒu bù wán de lù.
读不尽的书，走不完的路。

To have half-knowledge of ten things is not as good as thorough knowledge of just one.
(Better to master one thing than try to be a "Jack of all trades, master of none.")
Shí shì bàn tōng bùrú yí shì jīngtōng.
十事半通不如一事精通。

Learning has no boundaries.
Xué wú zhǐ jìng.
学无止境。—*Confucius*

Learning is like rowing a boat against the current; if you don't advance, you'll regress.
Nì shuǐ xíng zhōu, bú jìn zé tuì.
逆水行舟，不进则退。

Familiarity can engender skill.
(Practice makes perfect.)
Shú néng shēng qiǎo.
熟能生巧。

"A LITTLE LEARNING IS A DANGEROUS THING"

Better to go without books than to believe everything they say.
(Don't believe everything you read.)
Jìn xìn shū bù rú wú shū.
尽信书不如无书。

Learning without thinking is ignorance; thinking without learning (study) is dangerous.

Xué ér bùsī zé wǎng, sī ér bù xué zé dài.

学而不思则罔，思而不学则殆。

If you know [something], to recognize that you know it; and if you don't know [something], to realize that you don't know it—that is [true] knowledge.

Zhī zhī wéi zhī zhī bù zhī wéi bù zhī shì zhī yě.

知之为知之不知为不知是知也。—*Confucius*

[Don't be like] a frog at the bottom of a well.

(This proverb is based on an ancient fable of a frog that lived at the bottom of a well. He thought that the well was the entire world, until one day a sea turtle fell in and informed him of a much larger world outside the narrow confines of that well. The Chinese, as well as the Japanese, use this fable to describe people with a provincial, narrow-minded view of things due to ignorance.)

Jǐng dǐ zhī wā.

井底之蛙。

TRUE KNOWLEDGE

One can know the world without going outside. One can see the Way of Heaven without looking out the window.

Bù chū hù, zhī tiānxià; búkuì yǒu, jiàn tiān dào.

不出户，知天下；不窥牖，见天道。—*Lao Zi*

2 Patience and Perseverance

Traditional societies with long histories perhaps know the value of patience better than societies with much shorter histories. They understand that it often takes a long time to bring about the changes that you desire. The first saying below derives from the fact that in ancient China, except for the upper class, the majority of people often didn't have enough to eat. To become fat in traditional China, and indeed in almost every traditional society in the world, was a sign that you were prosperous enough to have an abundance of food. So being "fat" was a good thing!

The fourth proverb below refers to an ancient story about an old farmer who lived on one side of a huge mountain but whose fields were on the other side. Every morning, the old man and his sons had to go around the mountain to cultivate their crops. One day, the old man convinced his sons to start removing the mountain with their shovels. The man's neighbors naturally thought that the old man was crazy for having such a foolish notion and told him so. The old man replied that although the mountain could not be "moved" away in his lifetime or even that of his sons and grandsons, over time his family would eliminate this obstacle that made their lives difficult, if only they persevered. This realization of the need to be patient in achieving one's goals is not unknown outside China. Witness the expressions "Rome wasn't built in a day" and "Good things take time." But unlike in China, in the United States the focus is on achieving quick results, such as "learning Chinese in ten minutes a day" or wanting things to be "done yesterday." Americans sound like the farmer who wanted to help his crops grow faster by pulling on their stalks, which only ends up killing the plant. Older societies like China caution against such unreasonable expectations.

A fat person didn't get fat with just one mouthful.
(Rome wasn't built in a day.)
Pàngzi búshì yìkǒu chīde.
胖子不是一口吃的。

Food must be eaten bite by bite; a road must be walked step by step.
(Things must be accomplished one step at a time and cannot be rushed.)
Fàn yào yìkǒu yìkǒu de chī, lù děi yíbù yíbù de zǒu.
饭要一口一口地吃，路得一步一步地走。

One who is burning with impatience can never eat hot porridge.
(Patience is necessary to accomplish anything, even when it comes to waiting for your rice gruel to be heated.)
Xīn jí chībùdé rè zhōu.
心急吃不得热粥。

One who is burning with impatience can never eat hot porridge

心急吃不得热粥

The foolish old man moved the mountain.
(Anything can be done if you work long and hard enough at it.)
Yú gōng yí shān.
愚公移山。

With enough work, an iron rod can be ground into a needle.
(Almost anything can be achieved if you put enough effort into it.)
Zhǐyào gōngfu shēn, tiě chǔ móchéng zhēn.
只要功夫深，铁杵磨成针。

Good things are produced only through much grinding.
(Nothing good can be accomplished without a lot of work and many setbacks.)
Hǎo shì duō mó.
好事多磨。

Many little drops of water can turn into a [mighty] river.
(Giant oaks from tiny acorns grow.)
Juānjuān zhī dī huaì chéng jiānghé.
涓涓之滴汇成江河。

A thousand-mile journey starts under your feet.
(The longest journey begins with a single step.)
Qiān lǐ zhī lù shǐ yú zú xià.
千里之路始于足下。 —*Lao Zi*

Don't fear going slow [making slow progress]; just fear standing still.
Búpà màn, jiù pà zhàn.
不怕慢，就怕站。

[Don't] pull on seedlings to help them grow.
(It's human nature to be impatient for good things to happen, but you can't force good things to happen before the required time has elapsed.)
Bá miáo zhù zhǎng.
拔苗助长。

It takes one [full] year for a tree to start growing; it takes ten years for a person to start growing.
(Good things take time, especially for a person to mature into wisdom.)
Yìnián shù mù, shí nián shù rén.
一年树木，十年树人。

Failure is the mother of success.
Shībài shì chénggōng zhī mǔ.
失败是成功之母。

Everything is hard in the beginning.
Wàn shì qǐ tóu nán.
万事起头难。

3 Humility and Contentment

Every traditional culture has stressed the need for humility. Many centuries ago, the Christian Church in Europe posited the seven deadly sins, pride first among them. East Asian societies throughout their history have emphasized the virtue of humility more than most other societies.

For millennia, China has been one of the most densely populated countries in the world, as have Japan and Korea. Perhaps this is what caused the peoples of these three East Asian cultures to emphasize the good of the group over that of the individual. In a crowded society, where people lived in large communities side by side with their neighbors, a high priority was placed on maintaining social harmony. The need for humility was stressed to prevent that harmony from being disturbed by boastfulness and selfishness.

To this day, people in China, as well as in Japan and Korea, do not accept a compliment by saying "thank you," as we do in the West. Instead, the reply to every compliment is a set phrase such as "not at all, not at all" (*nǎlǐ, nǎlǐ* 哪里，哪里) or "I don't dare accept" (*bùgǎndāng* 不敢当). When someone invites guests to his home for a meal, in spite of the fact that the table will be groaning with dishes, the host will humbly declare, "There's nothing to eat" (*méi shénme cài* 没什么菜). Most important, Chinese and other Asians have been culturally trained to speak little about themselves or their accomplishments. This restraint extends to boasting about family members as well, because in China your family is an extension of yourself. So praising a family member is akin to praising oneself.

The Chinese have argued throughout the ages that having a humble attitude should encourage you to admit when you don't know something. They have also stressed that people should not pridefully compare themselves with others but modestly accept the fact that there will always be others who are superior to them in some way. The proverbs and sayings below all emphasize the importance of being humble, dating back to the words of Confucius 2,500 years ago. Contentment can only be found in not envying others or comparing yourself to them but in being satisfied with what you have.

Compare yourself to those who are superior to you, and you'll find yourself lacking; compare yourself to those who are inferior to you, and you'll find yourself more than good enough.
Bǐ shàng bùzú, bǐ xià yǒu yú.
比上不足，比下有余。—*Confucius*

If you compare yourself to others, it'll just get you angry.
Rén bǐ rén qìsǐ rén.
人比人气死人。

老王卖瓜，自卖自夸

Old Wang praises his own melons while he sells them

Looking from this mountain, that yonder mountain seems higher.

("The grass is always greener on the other side of the fence";
don't assume that others have it better than you do.)

Zhè shān wàngzhe nà shān gāo.

这山望着那山高。

Those who know that they have enough are always happy.

Zhī zú zhě cháng lè yě.

知足者常乐也。

Arrogance is the enemy of victory.

(Pride goeth before a fall.)

Jiāoào shì shènglì de dírén.

骄傲是胜利的敌人。

A great man is silent about his past glories.

(Truly great people never dwell on their past glories.)

Hǎo hàn bùtí dāngnián yǒng.

好汉不提当年勇。

The fool does not ask; he who asks is no fool.
(If you really want to learn, you have to be humble enough to ask questions and reveal your ignorance.)
Yú zhě bú wèn, wèn zhě bù yú.
愚者不问，问者不愚。—*Confucius*

If your face is ugly, you can't blame the mirror.
(If you have shortcomings, you have only yourself to blame, i.e., a poor workman always blames his tools.)
Liǎn chǒu guàibùzháo jìngzi.
脸丑怪不着镜子。

CAUTIONS AGAINST PRIDE AND BOASTING

However strong you are, there's always someone stronger; never brag about yourself to others.
(No matter how good you are at something, there's always someone better than you, so it's foolish to boast about your skill.)
Qiáng zhōng yèng yǒu qiáng zhōng shǒu, mò xiàng rén qián kuà dà kǒu.
强中更有强中手，莫向人前夸大口。

Beyond the sky is another sky; beyond the mountain is another mountain.
(No matter how great a person or a thing might be, there's always someone or something that's at least as great and perhaps even greater.)
Tiān wài yǒu tiān, shān wài yǒu shān.
天外有天，山外有山。

The moon waxes only to wane; water fills to the brim only to overflow.
(Success is always short-lived, so boastfulness is empty vanity.)
Yuè mǎn zé kuī, shuǐ mǎn zé yì.
月满则亏，水满则溢。

Wielding the ax in front of Ban's gate
(Trying to show off one's carpentry skills in front of the legendary master carpenter, Ban; performing in front of someone who is much more skilled than you are)
Bān mén nòng fǔ
班门弄斧

Old Wang praises his own melons while he sells them.
(He blows his own horn; said teasingly of those who boast of their own accomplishments)
Lǎo Wáng mài guā, zì mài zì kuà.
老王卖瓜，自卖自夸。

Good cats don't [constantly] meow, and good dogs don't [always] leap about.
(Truly talented people don't boast or show off.)
Hǎo māo bújiào, hǎo gǒu bútiào.
好猫不叫，好狗不跳。

A half-filled bottle makes noise [when shaken], while a full bottle makes none.
(Those who know the least boast the most, while the superior person remains silent.)
Yì píng bùxiǎng, bànpíng dīngdāng.
一瓶不响，半瓶叮当。

When you can't even put yourself to rights, how can you hope to transform others?
(We should work on making ourselves better instead of trying to improve other people.)
Bùnéng zhèng jǐ, yān néng huà rén.
不能正己，焉能化人。

If you don't talk about my bald head, I won't laugh at your poor eyesight.
(We shouldn't concentrate on the shortcomings of others when we each have some of our own.)
Nǐ shuōbùdé wǒ tóu tū, wǒ xiàobùdé nǐ yǎn xiā.
你说不得我头秃，我笑不得你眼瞎。

Those who retreated 50 paces [running away in battle] laugh at those who retreated 100 paces.
(That's the pot calling the kettle black.)
Wǔshí bù xiào yìbǎi bù.
五十步笑一百步。

A horse doesn't know its face is long; an ox doesn't know its horns are crooked.
(People rarely realize their own shortcomings.)
Mǎ bùzhī zìjǐ liǎn cháng, niú bùzhī zìjǐ jiǎo wān.
马不知自己脸长，牛不知自己角弯。

Talking

In a densely populated and group-oriented society like China, it has always been important to watch what one says so as not to risk offending one's neighbors. More significantly, China has always been an autocratic society under the control of a ruler with absolute power. The country was first ruled by kings, including in the time of Confucius, then by emperors from 221 BCE until 1911 CE. Then followed the dictatorial rule of Chiang Kai-shek from the 1920s until after World War II, and for the past six decades China has been under the rule of the Chinese Communist Party. This has meant that it has always been extremely dangerous to speak one's mind too freely, especially in challenging those in power.

Many centuries before dissidents were jailed under communist rule, legions of scholar-officials in ancient China were exiled or executed for speaking out in protest against injustice. One of the most beloved figures in Chinese history is the great poet and statesman of the eleventh century, Su Dongpo. Although he rose to high political office, becoming governor of a province and later an adviser to the emperor, he was exiled several times for criticizing government policy. He spent many of his later years in exile on the remote island of Hainan for bravely speaking out against reforms that he thought were harmful to the Chinese people.

It is, therefore, not surprising that many Chinese proverbs and sayings warn against expressing one's thoughts too freely. Below is but a sampling of cautionary advice when it comes to talk and speech.

CAUTIONS ABOUT SPEAKING

Sickness enters through the mouth; misfortune comes out of it.
(Loose lips sink ships.)
Bìng cóng kǒu rù, huò cóng kǒu chū.
病从口入，祸从口出。

The mouth and tongue have always been the roots of calamity.
Kǒu shé cónglái shì huò jī.
口舌从来是祸基。

The tongue is the source of both benefits and harm; the mouth is a door that opens to either disaster or blessings.
Shé wéi lì hài běn, kǒu shì huò fú mén.
舌为利害本，口是祸福门。

31

The tip of the tongue, though soft, can sting people

舌尖虽软能蜇人

The mouth is the door to disaster; the tongue is the knife that can kill you.

Kǒu shì huò zhī mén, shé wéi zhǎn shēn dāo.

口是祸之门，舌为斩身刀。

You only get criticized if you open your mouth too much; troubles all come from trying to show off.

Shìfēi zhǐ wèi duō kāikǒu, fánnǎo jiē yīn qiáng chūtóu.

是非只为多开口，烦恼皆因强出头。

Don't cross the river before rolling up your trouser legs; don't open your mouth before knowing the true state of things.

Bù juǎn kùjiǎo, bù guòhé; bùmō dǐxì, bù kāi qiāng.

不卷裤脚不过河；不摸底细不开腔。

About matters that don't concern you, don't open your mouth; when questioned, shake your head and say you know nothing about it.

(Don't comment on the affairs of others when they don't concern you.)

Bú gàn jǐ shì, bù zhāngkǒu; yíwèn yáotóu sānbùzhī.

不干己事，不张口；一问摇头三不知。

Close your mouth and hide your tongue, and you can settle down safely anywhere.

(Cautious speech will keep you safe from harm.)

Bì kǒu shēn cáng shé, ānshēn chùchù láo.

闭口深藏舌，安身处处牢。

A closed mouth keeps flies from flying in.

(If you keep your mouth shut, you can't get into trouble.)

Bìzhe de zuǐ fēibújìn cāngyīng.

闭着的嘴飞不进苍蝇。

Foolish people wag their tongues; wise people use their brains.

Chǔnrén jiáoshé; zhìzhě dòngnǎo.

蠢人嚼舌；智者动脑。

Don't eat excessive amounts of food; don't indulge in excessive talk.

Guòtóu de fàn bié chī, guòtóu de huà bié jiǎng.

过头的饭别吃，过头的话别讲。

When meeting people, say only 30% [of what you're thinking]; don't toss out everything that's in your mind.

Féng rén zhǐ shuō sān fēn huà, wèi kě quán pāo yípiàn xīn.

逢人只说三分话，未可全抛一片心。

GOSSIP AND SLANDER

You can hold other people's hands [down], but you can't get them to hold their tongues.
[lit.: What you can hold down is people's hands; what you can't suppress is other people's mouths.]
(You can't stop others from talking; secrets will eventually come out.)
Nádezhù de shì shǒu, yǎnbuzhù de shì kǒu.
拿得住的是手，掩不住的是口。

A tongue may weigh little, but it can crush a man.
(Gossip is a fearful thing that can do great harm.)
Shétóu dǐxià yāsǐ rén.
舌头底下压死人。

Who is never gossiped about behind his back, and who never gossips about people to others?
(No one is exempt from gossip, since everyone loves to talk about other people.)
Shéi rén bèi hòu wú rén shuō, nǎ ge rén qián bù shuō rén?
谁人背后无人说，哪个人前不说人？

Kind words need not be spoken behind people's backs; words spoken behind people's backs are rarely kind.
Hǎo huà bù bèi rén, bèi rén méi hǎo huà.
好话不背人，背人没好话。

It is preferable to believe there's some truth to a rumor than to believe that there's nothing there.
Níng kě xìn qí yǒu, bù kě xìn qí wú.
宁可信其有，不可信其无。

After something has passed through three mouths, even
snakes are said to have grown legs.
(Every rumor becomes exaggerated to a ridiculous point and is
not to be believed.)
Huà jīng sān zhāng zuǐ, cháng chóng yě zhǎng tuǐ.
话经三张嘴，长虫也长腿。

TACTFULNESS

In front of short people, do not speak about shortness.
(Don't hurt other people's feelings by speaking of their shortcomings in front of them.)
Dāngzhe ǎirén mò shuō duǎn huà.
当着矮人莫说短话。

Never hit a man in the face; never curse a man for his
weaknesses.
Dǎ rén bùdǎ liǎn, mà rén búmà duǎn.
打人不打脸，骂人不骂短。

People have a face [just as] a tree has bark.
(Never humiliate anyone or cause them to "lose face," or they
will feel vulnerable in the same way a tree becomes when it
loses its bark.)
Rén yǒu liǎn, shù yǒu pí.
人有脸，树有皮。

The tip of the tongue, though soft, can sting people.
Shé jiān suí ruǎn néng zhē rén.
舌尖虽软能蜇人。

不说不笑，不成世道

No talk and no laughter is no way to live

Cold rice and cold soup are easy to eat, [but] cold words and cold speech are hard to bear.
Lěng fàn lěng tāng hǎo chī, lěng yán lěng yǔ nán shòu.
冷饭冷烫好吃，冷言冷语难受。

Sweet words and pretty talk keep people warm for the three months of winter; cruel speech wounds people and leaves them cold for six months.
(Cruel words hurt us twice as much as kind words warm our hearts.)
Tián yán měi yǔ sān dōng nuǎn, è yǔ shāng rén liù yùe hán.
甜言美语三冬暖，恶语伤人六月寒。

CORRECT SPEECH

Dishes without salt are tasteless; words without reason are powerless.
(If you speak irrationally, you will most likely persuade no one.)
Cài méi yán, wú wèi; huà méi lǐ, wú lì.
菜没盐，无味；话没理，无力。

The truth is not always present in the loudest voice.
(Shouting does not prove you are in the right.)
Yǒulǐ búzài shēng gāo.
有理不在声高。

Once a word is spoken, even a team of four horses cannot catch up to it.
(A promise is a promise; the superior person keeps his word and never goes back on it.)
Yìyán jì chū, sì mǎ nán zhuī.
一言即出，驷马难追。

Speaking well is not as good as acting well.
(Actions speak louder than words.)
Shuōdehǎo bùrú zuòdehǎo.
说得好不如做得好。

HEED GOOD ADVICE

Good medicine may be bitter in the mouth, but will help you recover; honest advice may offend the ear, but will aid your conduct.
Liáng yào kǔ kǒu lì yú bìng, zhōng yán nì ěr lì yú xíng.
良药苦口利于病，忠言逆耳利于行。

Listening to the [good] advice of others, you will enjoy many hearty meals.
(If you learn from all the good advice others may give you, you'll get your fill of wisdom.)
Tīng rén quàn, chī bǎo fàn.
听人劝，吃饱饭。

Don't Forget to Laugh

No talk and no laughter is no way to live.
Bùshuō búxiào, bùchéng shìdào.
不说不笑，不成世道。

Cautions About Behavior in General

Ice that's three feet thick didn't form in just one cold day.
Bīng dòng sān chǐ fēi yírì zhī hán.
冰冻三尺非一日之寒。

To learn [to do] good requires three years, but to learn [to do] evil takes only three days.
(To become a truly moral person requires many years of cultivation, whereas it is all too easy to succumb to the baser impulses of human nature.)
Xué hǎo sān nián, xué huài sān tiān.
学好三年，学坏三天。

To protect against the cold, nothing is better than a heavy fur coat; to prevent slander, nothing is better than to refine your behavior.
(Moral conduct will protect you from reproach.)
Jiù hán mò rú zhòng qiú, zhǐ bàng mò rú zì xiū.
救寒莫如重裘，止谤莫如自修。

Never pull on your shoes in a melon patch; never adjust your cap under a plum tree.
(Avoid doing the slightest thing that might arouse suspicion that you've done something improper.)

Guā tián bú nà lǚ, lǐ xià bù zhěng guān.
瓜田不纳履，李下不整冠。

If you are patient in one moment of anger, you can escape a hundred days of sorrow [and regret].
Rěn yì shí zhī nù, kě miǎn bǎi rì zhī yōu.
忍一时之怒，可免百日之忧。

If you don't think three times before acting, you will have regret; if you restrain yourself in all things, you will have no worries.
Shì bù sān sī zhōng yǒu huǐ; rén néng bǎi rěn zì wú yōu.
事不三思终有悔；人能百忍自无忧。

A great person [has the courage to] accept the consequences of his own actions.
Hǎo hàn zuòshì hǎo hàn dāng.
好汉做事好汉当。

Each person should first clear away the snow from his own front door before worrying about the frost on his neighbor's roof.
(Your own problems are enough to handle without interfering in other people's affairs.)
Gè rén zì sǎo mén qián xuě, mò guǎn tā jiā wǎ shàng shuāng.
各人自扫门前雪，莫管他家瓦上霜。

If you go easy on others, they'll go easy on you

与人方便，自己方便

Don't fear a thousand-to-one chance that something bad might happen; fear the one chance in a thousand.
(We usually guard against the dangers we expect; it's the unlikely we must also guard against.)
Búpà yíwàn, zhǐ pà wànyī.
不怕一万，只怕万一。

A spear openly thrust at you is easy to dodge; an arrow shot from hiding is hard to defend against.
(Open attacks are easier to defend against than unexpected attacks from an unknown foe.)
Míng qiāng yì duǒ, àn jiàn nán fáng.
明枪易躲，暗箭难防。

Never harm another, but beware of others who may intend to harm you.
(Never harbor the intention to do harm to others, but be aware that others may harbor the intention to harm you.)
Hài rén zhī xīn bù kě yǒu, fáng rén zhī xīn bù kě wú.
害人之心不可有，防人之心不可无。

It's difficult to fathom what lies in people's hearts; it's hard to plumb the depths of the water in the ocean.

Rén xīn nán cè, hǎi shuǐ nán liáng.

人心难测，海水难量。

If you go easy on others, they'll go easy on you.

(If you aren't overly critical of the behavior of others, they will be more likely to not give you a hard time.)

Yǔ rén fāngbiàn, zìjǐ fāngbiàn.

与人方便，自己方便。

When you should let others off the hook, you must let them off the hook; when you should pardon others, you had best pardon them.

(Be lenient whenever possible, with the implication that others then will tend to show you leniency.)

Děi fàngshǒu shí xū fàngshǒu; děi ráo rén chù qiě ráo rén.

得放手时须放手；得饶人处且饶人。

Never use your influence completely; never show off your wealth completely; never take advantage completely; never display your cleverness completely.

(As Confucius cautioned, "follow the principle of the Golden Mean" and show moderation in all things; to do otherwise is to open yourself up to resentment and envy and eventual harm.)

Shì bùkě shǐ jìn, fú bùkě xiǎng jìn, piányi bùkě zhān jìn, cōngmíng bùkě yòng jìn.

势不可使尽，福不可享尽，便宜不可占尽，聪明不可用尽。

Morality

For about the past 1,500 years, Buddhism has been the dominant religion in China. Like other great world religions, Buddhism preaches that one should not kill, steal, slander, or harm his fellow human beings in any way. It is a religion that emphasizes compassion and self-abnegation. The Eightfold Path formulated by Buddha as the way people should live their lives has a lot in common with the Ten Commandments in the Bible. The most popular form of Buddhism pictured a heavenly paradise as well as a hell with even more horrific torments than Dante describes in his "Inferno." However, Buddhism never sought to amass the power that the medieval Church wielded in the West, nor did it enforce its morality over the people the way ecclesiastical authorities in the West did for centuries.

In fact, it has not been Buddhist morality that has had the largest influence on Chinese culture over the ages but, rather, the moral teachings of Confucius. It was Confucius who, five centuries before Jesus, posited the "Golden Rule," albeit in the negative, when he said, "Do not do to others what you would not want done to yourself." In *The Analects*, the book that records his teachings, the ancient sage talked about his ideal human relationships. He preached virtues such as righteousness, justice, respect, kindness, and reciprocity. Books based on his teachings became the canon of Chinese thought and the basis of Chinese education for nearly two thousand years. Every scholar had to study these classics in order to pass the imperial examinations to become an official. To this day, Confucian ideals and morality continue to influence not only the people of China but those in Japan and Korea as well.

The third school of thought in ancient China also had something to say about morality—Taoism. While Confucius was concerned with human relationships in this world, Buddhism concentrated on the afterlife and the nature of life itself. More a complement than a rival to those other two philosophies, Taoism, as expressed by the ancient philosophers Lao Zi and Zhuang Zi, encouraged people to become attuned to nature and to live simple lives in harmony with the Tao, the Way (of Nature).

The three schools of thought described above all generated the following maxims regarding moral behavior. Many of these are popular sayings: expressions by the common people of the morality they had absorbed from their culture.

Do No Harm to Others

The highest form of doing good is like water; water benefits all things but does seek anything (for itself).
Shàng shàn ruò shuǐ, shuǐ shàn lì wàn wù ér bù zhēng.
上善若水，水善利万物而不争。 —*Lao Zi*

纸里包不住火

You can't conceal fire by wrapping it in paper

What you do not want done to you, do not do to other people.

(Do not do unto others what you would not wish to be done to you.)

Jǐ suǒ búyù wù shī yú rén.

己所不欲勿施于人。—*Confucius*

THE MORAL PERSON

A superior person knows what is moral; a petty person [only] knows what is profitable.

Jūnzǐ yù yú yì, xiǎo rén yù yú lì.

君子喻于义，小人喻于利。

Saving a life is better than building a seven-story pagoda.

(Helping others in a concrete way is more important than trying to show one's goodness by building a temple.)

Jiù rén yímìng shèng zào qījí fútú.

救人一命胜造七级浮屠。

[If you] plant melons, [you] reap melons; [if you] plant beans, [you] reap beans.
(You reap what you sow.)
Zhòng guā dé guā, zhòng dòu dé dòu.
种瓜得瓜，种豆得豆。

Better to be a broken piece of jade than an unbroken shard of clay tile.
(Better to die with honor than live with dishonor.)
Nìng wéi yù suì,bù wéi wǎ quán.
宁为玉碎，不为瓦全。

Real gold does not fear the furnace.
(A person's true character is revealed in adversity.)
Zhēn jīn búpà huǒ.
真金不怕火。

THE CONSEQUENCES OF WRONGDOING

Onc false step can cause life-long regret.
Yī shī zú chéng qiān gǔ hèn.
一失足成千古恨。

Hit someone, and you'll worry for three days [i.e., a long time]; curse someone, and you'll feel ashamed for three days.
(Improper conduct will only lead to regret and worry.)
Dǎ rén sān rì yōu, mà rén sān rì xiū.
打人三日忧，骂人三日羞。

No matter how big your hands may be, they can't cover the whole sky

手大遮不过天

If you do nothing shameful during the day, there's no need to fear ghosts will come knocking at your door at night.
(If your behavior is moral and upright, you'll sleep with a clear conscience.)
Báitiān búzuò kuīxīn shì, yèlǐ búpà guǐ qiāo mén.
白天不做亏心事，夜里不怕鬼敲门。

Good will be rewarded with good, and evil will be rewarded with evil; it may not yet have happened, but that's only because the time has not yet come.
Shàn yǒu shàn bào, è yǒu è bào, búshì búbào, shíchén wèi dào.
善有善报，恶有恶报，不是不报，时辰未到。

Wrongdoing Is Always Discovered and Punished Eventually

Heaven's net is vast; it's cast far and wide, but lets nothing through.
(No one escapes justice.)
Tiān wǎng huīhuī, shū ér búlòu.
天网恢恢，疏而不漏。

You can't conceal fire by wrapping it in paper.
(The truth will out; no wrongdoing can be concealed for long.)
Zhǐ lǐ bāobuzhù huǒ.
纸里包不住火。

No matter how big your hands may be, they can't cover the whole sky.
(You might be able to hide your wrong-doing for a while, but eventually the truth will be known.)
Shǒu dà zhēbuguò tiān.
手大遮不过天。

A monk may run away, but his temple can't run away.
(You may try to escape punishment for your wrongdoing, but eventually the authorities will find and catch you by knowing your family and workplace.)
Pǎole héshàng pǎobùliǎo miào.
跑了和尚跑不了庙。

Good things [about people] rarely make it out the door; bad things are broadcast for a thousand miles.
(People far prefer to spread rumors of evildoing much more than they care to convey news of good deeds.)
Hǎo shì bù chū mén, è shì chuán qiān lǐ.
好事不出门，恶事传千里。

If you don't want people to know [the wrong you did], then it's best not to do it.
Ruò yào rén bù zhī, chú fēi jǐ mò wéi.
若要人不知，除非己莫为。

酒后无德

After too much wine, there is no virtue

AVOID TEMPTATION

Walk often by the river's edge, and your shoes are bound to get wet.
(A person with the power to grant favors will likely give in to the temptation to be bribed.)
Cháng zài hé biān zǒu, nǎ néng bù shī xié.
常在河边走，哪能不湿鞋。

After [too much] wine, there is no virtue.
(Alcohol leads to immorality.)
Jiǔ hòu wú dé.
酒后无德。

If you don't eat fish, your mouth won't smell fishy.
(If you do nothing morally questionable, you'll stay out of trouble.)
Bù chī yú, kǒu bù xīng.
不吃鱼，口不腥。

The sea of suffering is boundless, [but] if you turn around you'll spy the shore.

(It is never too late to repent; if someone on the wrong path in life mends his ways, he will find the path of salvation.)

Kǔ hǎi wú biān, huí tóu shì àn.

苦海无边，回头是岸。

If the butcher lays down his knife, he has but to stand to become a Buddha [a saint].

(Any wrongdoer can achieve salvation as soon as he renounces evil.)

Fàng xià tú dāo, lì dì chéng fó.

放下屠刀，立地成佛。

6 Money

Buddhism taught that people would find relief from the suffering in human existence only if they ceased to desire things like money and fame. Confucius exhorted people to be high-minded and moral rather than to seek petty profit for themselves. The Chinese, however, have always been a very pragmatic people. Regardless of what Chinese religion and philosophy warned about the pursuit of wealth, most Chinese have long since realized that, while money might not be able to buy happiness or love, it can buy nearly everything else.

Traditionally, at the time of the new year, the most important Chinese holiday, people greet one another with the time-honored phrase: "*Gōngxǐ fācái!*" (恭喜发财, "Congratulations, and may you become wealthy!"). In southern dialects the word for the number eight is pronounced the same as *fā* in the expression *fācái* (to become wealthy), so many Chinese in Hong Kong or Guangdong pay extra for phone numbers and car license plates with as many eights in them as possible. In addition, in southern dialects the word for the number one is homophonous with *yào* (will), so phone numbers or license plates such as 1818, which is pronounced like *yàofā, yàofā* (will get rich, will get rich) are highly desirable. Phone numbers, license plate numbers, and addresses with these numbers are sure to bring them wealth and good fortune, or so many Chinese believe.

Around 1980, when the Chinese Communist government began to espouse the introduction of capitalism in what had been a purely socialist economy, the country's leader, Deng Xiaoping, supposedly initiated this radical change of direction by stating: "To get rich is glorious." The rapid increase in the number of millionaires in China today attests to the fact that many Chinese have followed Deng's advice.

And yet most of the popular sayings about money in Chinese culture are from the common people of previous centuries. They keenly felt the pain of poverty and realized only too well what the lack of money meant in their lives.

Money allows you to speak with the gods.
(Money is power.)
Qián néng tōng shén.
钱能通神。

With money, you can even get the devil to push the millstone for you.
(Money makes everything possible.)
Yǒu qián néng shǐ guǐ tuī mò.
有钱能使鬼推磨。

Money resolves all matters just as a fire roasts a pig's head.
Qián dào gōng shì bàn, huǒ dào zhū tóu làn.
钱到公事办，火到猪头烂。

With money, you can even get the devil to push the millstone for you

有钱能使鬼推磨

Government office doors everywhere face south; without money, it's useless to enter even if you're in the right.
Tiānxià yámén cháo nán kāi, yǒu lǐ wú qián mò jìnlái.
天下衙门朝南开，有理无钱莫进来。

A poor man's ambition stops short; a thin horse's mane appears long.
(Poverty stifles ambition.)
Rén qióng zhì duǎn, mǎ shòu máo cháng.
人穷志短，马瘦毛长。

A poor man can stand by the roadside, but no one will ask how he is; a rich man can hide deep in the mountains, but distant relatives will come visit.
Qióng zài lù biān wú rén wèn, fù zài shēn shān yǒu yuǎn qīn.
穷在路边无人问，富在深山有远亲。

People die in pursuit of wealth; birds die in pursuit of food.
(Greed can lead to one's demise.)
Rén wèi cái sǐ, niǎo wèi shí wáng.
人为财死，鸟为食亡。

**Always remember in times of plenty the days when you had
nothing; don't wait until you're poor again to recall fondly
the times of plenty.**

(When you do have money, remember the days when you were
poor and be frugal, or you'll wind up poor again, wistfully re-
calling your days of wealth.)

Cháng jiāng yǒu rì sī wú rì, mò dài wú rì sī yǒu shí.

常将有日思无日，莫待无日思有时。

**When there's no wine [left] in the pot, it's hard to get your
guests to stay.**

(If you have no money, it's hard to find friends.)

Hú zhōng wú jiǔ nán liú kè.

壶中无酒难留客。

**It's common for people to add flowers to adorn [your] bro-
cade [robe], but in snowy weather how many will send you
charcoal [to heat your home]?**

(It's easy to find fair-weather friends, but a friend in need is a
friend, indeed.)

Jǐn shàng tiān huā cháng shí yǒu; xuě zhōng sòng tàn néng jǐ rén?

锦上添花常时有；雪中送炭能几人。

[If you pay] one cent, [you get] one cent of merchandise.

(You get what you pay for.)

Yìfēn qián yìfēn huò.

一分钱一分货。

Cheap things aren't good, and good things aren't cheap.

Piányi méi hǎo huò, hǎo huò bù piányi.

便宜没好货，好货不便宜。

Expensive things aren't really expensive; cheap things aren't really cheap.

(Buy cheap, get cheap; expensive things tend to last a long time and so are a better bargain in the end, while cheap things quickly become useless because they're poorly made.)

Guìde búguì, jiànde bújiàn.

贵的不贵，贱的不贱。

[The lack of] one penny can worry to death even the bravest of heroes.

(Even the most heroic person fears having no money when in need.)

Yìwén qián jísǐ yīngxióng hàn.

一文钱急死英雄汉。

7 Conformity

In the West, particularly in the United States, individuality is glorified, as are competition and fame, a heritage of the American experience in which self-reliance was a virtue for the pioneers in settling the frontier. In such a society, which protects the right to be different, many people seek the rewards that come from "sticking out" in a crowd. By contrast, in China, with a long history as a settled, highly populated society, people have always mistrusted and even feared fame or of sticking out in a crowd. That is because calling attention to oneself too often resulted in misfortune. At the very least, being superior or different in any way can arouse jealousy among those who are less fortunate. At worst, a famous or individualistic person can easily become the victim of malicious and harmful gossip.

As a country of immigrants, the United States has the most heterogeneous society in the world, while China is among the most homogeneous. While the United States and other Western countries have had a fairly long history of democracy, China's government has always been hierarchical, ruled by an autocratic authority. All these factors have contributed to making Chinese society prize social harmony more than the rights of

锅里满才能碗里满

Only when the wok is full can people's bowls be filled

the individual. The great variety of Chinese sayings that warn against the danger of calling attention to oneself or of showing off is a manifestation of the degree to which China, among other Asian societies, has tended to be conformist and group-oriented.

It's significant that Japan has similar sayings that advise conformity rather than individuality. Among the most famous of these is: "The nail that sticks up gets hammered down." English has no equivalent sayings. Instead, it features expressions like "The squeaky wheel gets the grease." The implication is the opposite of the Chinese and Japanese sayings—that calling attention to oneself is likely to have a positive outcome.

When trees are big [tall], they invite the wind [to knock them down].
Shù dà zhāo fēng.
树大招风。

The bird that sticks its head out is the first to get shot.
Qiāngdǎ chū tóu niǎo.
枪打出头鸟。

The rafter that sticks out is the first to rot.
Chū tóu de chuánzi xiān làn.
出头的椽子先烂。

People fear getting famous; pigs fear getting fat.
Rén pà chū míng, zhū pà zhuàng.
人怕出名，猪怕壮。

WORK FOR THE BENEFIT OF THE GROUP RATHER THAN YOUR OWN INDIVIDUAL SELFISH DESIRES

Only when the water in the big river is high will the small streams rise.
(An individual's well-being depends on collective prosperity.)
Dà hé yǒu shuǐ xiǎo hé mǎn.
大河有水小河满。

Only when the wok is full can [people's] bowls be filled.
(Only when the group prospers, be it the family, the community, or the entire society, can the individual prosper.)
Guō lǐ mǎn cái néng wǎn lǐ mǎn.
锅里满才能碗里满。

STRENGTH LIES IN UNITY

A single thread cannot make a cord; a lone tree cannot make a forest.
Dān sī bù chéng xiàn, gū mù bù chéng lín.
单丝不成线，孤木不成林。

When people are of one mind, they can fill in the oceans and move mountains.

(In unity there is strength.)

Rén xīn qí, hǎi kě tián, shān kě yí.

人心齐，海可填，山可移。

If everyone is of one mind, yellow dirt can be made into gold.

(Almost anything can be accomplished if people work together.)

Dàjiā yì tiáo xīn, huáng tǔ biànchéng jīn.

大家一条心，黄土变成金。

There is strength in numbers; more firewood makes a bigger fire.

Rén duō lìliàng dà, chái duō huǒyàn gāo.

人多力量大，柴多火焰高。

A peony in bloom is a lovely thing, but it still needs the green leaves to support it.

(No man is an island; even the finest or most capable person needs the help of others.)

Mùdān huāér suī hǎo, hái yào lǜ yèér fúchí.

牡丹花儿虽好，还要绿叶儿扶持。

Age

Unlike in contemporary Western society, where youth is glorified and old age is something to be lamented, traditional societies and particularly China revered the elderly. In ancient times, when there was little technological innovation or change from one generation to the next, the older you were, the more you knew about life, simply because you had experienced so much more than the young.

Old age was revered to such an extent in ancient China that people wanted to advance their age as soon as possible. To that end, traditionally children were said to be "one year old" on the day they were born, and at the New Year they would gain another year of age. Therefore, if you happened to be born on the day before the Chinese New Year, usually sometime in February, you would be considered two years old when, by Western reckoning, you might only be two days old!

In fact, the Chinese word for "old" (*lǎo* 老), has none of the negative connotations of the English word. *Lǎo* literally means "venerably aged" and includes the notion of respect.

While most of the proverbs and sayings below do reflect respect for the wisdom that comes with age, a few other popular

People fear being poor in old age; rice fears a cold wind in late autumn

人怕老来穷，禾怕寒露风

maxims argue that the elderly are not always wiser for having lived longer.

The largest number of sayings about age and aging, however, have nothing to do with wisdom or lack of it but, rather, with mortality—an experience that is unavoidable in every culture.

AGING AND MORTALITY

At three years old, you can see the person when grown; at seven years old, you can see the person when old.
(The child is father to the man; our personalities are already evident in childhood.)
Sān suì kàn dà, qī suì kàn lǎo.
三岁看大，七岁看老。

In the mountains, there are often trees a thousand years old, but there are few people in the world who are one hundred years old.
Shān zhōng cháng yǒu qiān nián shù, shìshàng bìng wú bǎisuì rén.
山中常有千年树，世上并无百岁人。

People die like an [oil] lamp going out.
Rén sǐ rú dēng miè.
人死如灯灭。

An old person when healthy is like a chilly spring or a late autumn warm spell.
(Nothing lasts very long.)
Lǎo jiàn chūn hán qiū hòu rè.
老健春寒秋后热。

People live only one lifetime, just as grass grows for only one autumn.
Rén shēng yíshì, cǎo shēng yì qiū.
人生一世，草生一秋。

How many times in one's life can you see the moon overhead?
(Life is brief, so how many times can we experience good times?)
Rén shēng jǐ jiàn yuè dāng tóu?
人生几见月当头？

The springtime of one's life passes quickly, and white hair is hard to avoid.
(Our youth passes quickly, and old age comes all too soon.)
Qīngchūn yì guò, bái fǎ nán ráo.
青春易过，白发难饶。

If you don't work hard when you're young and strong, you'll lead a miserable life when old.
Shào zhuàng bù nǔlì, lǎodà tú shāng bēi.
少壮不努力，老大徒伤悲。

生姜还是老的辣

Ginger gets spicier with age

If you don't have a long-range plan for the future, you'll find yourself with nothing in old age.
Rén wú qiān rì jì, lǎo zhì yìchǎng kōng.
人无千日计，老至一场空。

Having aspirations has nothing to do with your age; without aspirations, you may live a hundred years for no purpose.
Yǒu zhì búzài nián gāo, wú zhì kōng huó bǎi suì.
有志不在年高，无志空活百岁。

PEOPLE OFTEN DO GET BETTER WITH AGE

Trees, when old, have more roots; people, when old, have more life experience.
Shù lǎo gēn duō, rén lǎo jiànshí duō.
树老根多，人老见识多。

We only sleep best right before dawn; people learn wisdom only in old age.
Shí dào tiān liàng fāng hǎo shuì, rén dào lǎo lái cái xué guāi.
时到天亮方好睡，人到老来才学乖。

If you want [to do things] well, ask the old [for advice].
Ruò yào hǎo, wèn sān lǎo.
若要好，问三老。

Ginger gets spicier with age.
(The older the violin, the sweeter the music; with old age can come wisdom)
Shēng jiāng háishì lǎode là.
生姜还是老的辣。

An old general who rides out on his horse [to battle] is worth any two others.
(An older person with experience is better at getting a job done than two young and inexperienced people.)
Lǎo jiàng chū mǎ, yígè dǐng liǎ.
老将出马，一个顶俩。

An old horse knows the way.
(Wisdom often comes with age.)
Lǎo mǎ shí tú.
老马识途。

THE PROBLEMS OF OLD AGE

When horses get old, no one rides them; when people get old, they are taken for a ride.
Mǎ lǎo wú rén qí, rén lǎo yǒu rén qī.
马老无人骑，人老有人欺。

Before you reach the age of 88, don't laugh at those who are lame or blind.

(We, too, someday may suffer the same fate as those we now find pitiable.)

Wèi dào bāshíbā, bùkě xiào rén jiǎo qué, yǎn xiā.

未到八十八，不可笑人脚瘸，眼瞎。

People fear being poor in old age; rice fears a cold wind in late autumn.

Rén pà lǎo lái qióng, hé pà hán lù fēng.

人怕老来穷，禾怕寒露风。

People fear their minds [and spirits] getting old, as trees fear their roots becoming old.

Rén pà lǎo xīn, shù pà lǎo gēn.

人怕老心，树怕老根。

When people grow old or pearls become yellow [with age], there is no medicine to cure them.

Rén lǎo zhū huáng méi yào yī.

人老珠黄没药医。

9 Time

Given our mortality, the older a person lives, the more he or she will come to realize that it is time, not money, that is our most precious treasure. The Chinese may have emphasized that fact more than most other cultures. Here are some of the best statements of how fleeting life is, and, therefore, how it is all the more to be valued. Some of the sayings also reflect the insights about the subjective way in which we perceive the passage of time, fast or slow, depending on our feelings at a particular moment.

An ounce of gold can't buy an ounce of time.
(Time is more valuable than money.)
Yícùn guāngyīn yícùn jīn, cùn jīn nán mǎi cùn guāngyīn.
一寸光阴一寸金，寸金难买寸光阴。

Gold lost may be found somewhere; time lost is nowhere to be found.
(You may recover money you've lost, but you can never recover lost time.)
Shīluò huángjīn yǒu chù zhǎo; shīluò guāngyīn wú chù xún.
失落黄金有处找；失落光阴无处寻。

An opportunity can't be missed; if lost, it will never come again

机不可失，失不再来

A hundred years of age is like a traveler passing by.

(Life is short and fleeting.)

Bǎi suì guāngyīn rú guò kè.

百岁光阴如过客。

One day of not seeing [a dear one seems] like three autumns.

(One day apart from those we love seems like three years; absence makes the heart grow fonder.)

Yírì bújiàn rú gé sānqiū.

一日不见如隔三秋。

When seeing off close friends and relations, the road seems [too] short; when returning to one's home, the road seems [too] long.

Sòng qīn de lù duǎn; huán xiāng de lù cháng.

送亲的路短；还乡的路长。

When you're enjoying yourself, you complain the night is too short; when you are lonely, you lament that each hour is so long.

(Time passes quickly when you're having a good time, but slowly when you're unhappy.)

Huānlè xián yè duǎn, jìmò hèn gēng cháng.
欢乐嫌夜短，寂寞恨更长。

When seeing off a dear friend, there must finally be a farewell.
(All good things come to an end; usually said in parting from a friend.)
Sòng jūn qiān lǐ, zhōng xū yì bié.
送君千里，终须一别。

(Even) sumptuous feasts must end (eventually).
(All good things come to an end; nothing lasts forever.)
Shèng yàn bì sàn.
盛宴必散。

No flower stays red for a hundred days.
(No flower blooms for long; nothing gold can stay.)
Huā wú bǎi rì hóng.
花无百日红。

The seasons yield to no one.
(Time waits for no man; all things must be done at the proper time.)
Jìjié bú ràng rén.
季节不让人。

An opportunity can't be missed; if lost, it will never come again.
(Opportunity knocks but once.)
Jī bù kě shī, shī búzài lái.
机不可失，失不再来。

花无百日红

No flower stays red for a hundred days

Do not spend the whole day in idleness; your youth will never come again.

Báirì mò xián guò, qīngchūn bú zài lái.

白日莫闲过，青春不再来。

If you fail to plan far into the future, you'll soon have worries in the near term.

Rén wú yuǎn lǜ, bì yǒu jìn yōu.

人无远虑, 必有近忧。

The whole year's plan depends on a good start in spring; the whole day's work depends on a good start at dawn.

(Do not procrastinate, but use your time wisely from the beginning.)

Yì nián zhī jì zàiyú chūn; yírì zhī jì zàiyú chén.

一年之计在于春； 一日之计在于晨。

10 Friends

Friendship is valued in every culture, but in few other cultures can one find the depth of friendship that has always been prevalent in China. Confucius spoke of five cardinal relationships, namely, those between ruler and subject, husband and wife, parents and children, older and younger siblings, and between friends. The first four of these major relationships were hierarchical; only the last was a relationship between equals. Because the bonds of friendship were prioritized by Confucius well over two thousand years ago, it is no wonder that this relationship is particularly emphasized in Chinese culture.

The Chinese poetry written in the Tang and Song dynasties, from the seventh century to the thirteenth century, is among the greatest in world literature. Much of it concerns the sorrow felt by the poet at having to part from a close friend, after one of them has been assigned an official post in a far-off part of the empire. In Western culture, where romantic love has been glorified, the love between a man and a woman was considered the closest bond. In traditional China, however, it was the relationship between two male friends that was usually the stronger emotional bond.

To this day in China, with women as well as men, much more

If you want to be a good person, seek good people as friends

要做好人，须寻好友

is expected from a friend than is usually true in the West. The Chinese make fewer friends, but they tend to keep them for life. The sacrifices of time and money that Chinese friends will make for one another often go far beyond what is expected or accepted in Western society. As a result, over the years the Chinese have produced some moving statements about the quality of friendship, while at the same time warning about "fair-weather friends."

TRUE FRIENDS ARE A TREASURE

In this world if one has a friend who understands you, that friend seems near even in the farthest corners of the earth.
(The greatest distances cannot separate close friends, whom you carry in your heart.)
Hǎi nèi cún zhī jǐ, tiān yá ruò bǐ lín.
海内存知己，天涯若比邻。

When your hair is in disarray, look for a comb; when your heart is in disarray, look for a friend.
Fǎ luàn zhǎo shūzi, xīn luàn zhǎo péngyou.
发乱找梳子，心乱找朋友。

It's easier to obtain a thousand ounces of gold than to find one person who really understands you.

Qiān jīn yì dé, zhī yīn nán qiú.

千金易得，知音难求。

To make friends, share your true thoughts and feelings, to make flowers grow, you must water their roots.

(To make friends, sincerity is most important.)

Jiāo rén jiāo xīn, jiāo huā jiāo gēn.

交人交心，浇花浇根。

The friendship between two superior people is clear as shallow water; interaction between petty people is sweet as honey.

(True friendship is transparent and not muddied by selfishness; relationships between petty people are superficially honey-tongued but lack sincerity.)

Jūnzǐ zhī jiāo dàn rú shuǐ, xiǎo rén zhī jiāo tián rú mì.

君子之交淡如水， 小人之交甜如蜜。

THE NATURE OF FRIENDSHIP

If water is too clear [and pure], you can't raise fish.

(You can't be too trivial or too inflexible about small matters. Compromise is often required to get what you want.)

Shuǐ qīng bùyǎng yú.

水清不养鱼。

不知其人，观其友

If you don't know someone, look carefully at his friends

Enjoy together the happy times and face together times of trouble.

(What friends should do, namely, stick together through thick and thin)

Yǒu fú tóng xiǎng, yǒu nàn tóng dāng.

有福同享，有难同当。

A thousand friends are too few, but one enemy is too many.

Péngyou qiānge shǎo, chóu rén yígè duō.

朋友千个少，仇人一个多。

Gain a friend, and you gain one more path [away from worry]; lose an enemy, and you've lost one more obstacle [in your way].

Duō yíge péngyou duō yìtiáo lù, shǎo yíge chóurén shǎo yìdǔ qiáng.

多一个朋友多一条路，少一个仇人少一堵墙。

When drinking with a kindred spirit, a thousand cups of wine seem too few; when conversing with an incompatible person, half a sentence seems too much.

Jiǔ féng zhī jǐ qiān bēi shǎo, huà bù tóu jī bàn jù duō.

酒逢知己千杯少，话不投机半句多。

At home, rely on your parents; outside your door, rely on your friends.

Zài jiā kào fùmǔ, chūmén kào péngyou.

在家靠父母，出门靠朋友。

If you want to be a good person, seek good people as friends.

Yào zuò hǎo rén, xū xún hǎo yǒu.

要做好人，须寻好友。

If you hang around vermilion pillars, you'll turn red; if you hang around ink, you'll turn black.

(You are influenced by the company you keep.)

Jìn zhū zhě chì, jìn mò zhě hēi.

近朱者赤，近墨者黑。

If you don't know someone, look carefully at his friends.

(People are judged by the company they keep.)

Bù zhī qí rén, guān qí yǒu.

不知其人，观其友。

11 Family

The family is the basic unit of society. But arguably few societies in the history of the world have placed as large an emphasis on its importance and defined so carefully the nature of the relationships within it as that of China. For most of their history, the Chinese have lived in large extended families. When the sons of the family married, they would bring their bride to live with their parents and raise their children in their ancestral home. In the complex families that resulted, the relationships between the various family members, including parents and children, elder and younger brothers, husbands and wives, and so on, were all governed by social protocol, and there were distinct terms for each family member. To this day Chinese lacks a singular term for "brother" or "sister," let alone "siblings." Relationships like this were too important to employ such generic terms. Instead they use the more specific terms "older brother" (*gēgē* 哥哥) and "younger brother" (*dìdì* 弟弟) and "older sister" (*jiějiě* 姐姐) and "younger sister" (*mèimèi* 妹妹) to emphasize each person's role in the family. Similarly, there is no generic word for "uncle"; rather, there are three, depending on whether your "uncle" is your father's older brother or younger brother or your mother's older or younger brother. And there are eight words for "cousin," depending on whether your "cousin" is older or younger than you, male or female, and on your father's or mother's side of the family. The specific terms by which you refer to your family members reflect the nature of the relationship that you are expected to have with them. Whenever a society places special importance on something within their culture, they develop specific terms for it rather than use a generic one. Thus the family and the relationships within it have been deemed so vital in the Chinese culture that the Chinese language has no fewer than 460 separate terms for family members!

As mentioned in the chapter on Friends, three of the five cardinal relationships posited by Confucius were within the family: between parents and children (specifically fathers and sons), husband and wife, and older brother and younger brother. In each of those three relationships, the former were to be obeyed and respected by the latter, whom they in turn were expected to nurture and care for. Marriages were commonly arranged by the families until the Chinese Communist Party outlawed such forced marriages in 1954. Yet many married couples did come to love one another, as can be seen in some of the sayings below on the subject of marriage.

Children were expected to be respectful and obedient to their parents as well as to care for them in their old age. After all, children owed the gift of life to their father and mother, and this meant that they had to spend their lives repaying that gift. There is no adequate term in English to fully convey the weight of the Chinese concept that translates as "filial piety"—namely, this obligation to respect and care for one's parents not just in this life but in the next. The latter part of this responsibility refers to the burning of paper money and the saying of prayers for the repose

To give a child a thousand pieces of gold is not as good as giving him a skill

赐子千金不如赐子一艺

of the souls of their dead parents, a custom that dates back more than several millennia.

Having children—preferably sons—to take care of you and to carry on the family line is considered the highest virtue in Chinese society. To this day, the word for "good/fine/well/O.K." is *hǎo* (好), the character for which shows a woman and a child together. When the Chinese Communist Party instituted the "one-child policy" starting around 1980, it was difficult at first to convince the Chinese people to limit the number of their children to one in the cities and two in the countryside, given this emphasis on the importance of having children. In time, the vast majority of Chinese came to see such a draconian policy as necessary for advancing their standard of living. A large percentage of the Chinese population has come to appreciate the better life that they can give their only child, and the great majority no longer oppose the policy as they did in the early years. Certainly, the policy has only made them value their children all the more. In recent years the government has quietly begun to relax this strict policy.

Confucius preached that a society could be harmonious and well-ordered only if the individual families that comprised that society were harmonious and well-ordered. Here are but a few of the many sayings that focus on relationships within the family. Their similarity to the way these relationships were viewed in traditional Western society merely affirms once again the common humanity of all people in the world.

THE FAMILY

If the family lives in harmony, everything will go well for them.
Jiā hé wàn shì xīng.
家和万事兴。

Even a family with a thousand people can only have one master.
Jiā yǒu qiān kǒu, zhǔ shì yì rén.
家有千口，主事一人。

Every family's classic saga has pages that are difficult to read.
(Every family has its own problems and difficult issues to deal with.)
Jiā jiā yǒu běn nán niàn de jīng.
家家有本难念的经。

Do not display to others your family's ugly problems.
(Don't air your dirty linen in public; don't discuss private problems with outsiders.)
Jiā chǒu bù kě wài yáng .
家丑不可外扬。

If you're not members of the same family, you won't enter by that family's door.
(It's not surprising that people in the same family should share the same opinions or habits.)
Búshì yì jiā rén bújìn yìjiā mén.
不是一家人不进一家门。

One raises children to provide against old age, just as one stores grain to provide against famine.
(Children are one's security in old age.)
Yǎng ér fáng lǎo, jī gǔ fáng jī.
养儿防老，积谷防饥。

A child will never look down on its mother as homely; a dog will never despise its master as poor.
Ér bù xián mǔ chǒu, gǒu bù xián zhǔ pín.
儿不嫌母丑，狗不嫌主贫。

When in a stable to buy a horse, take a good look at its mother.
(The apple doesn't fall far from the tree; like mother, like child.)
Cáotóu mǎi mǎ kàn mǔzi.
槽头买马看母子。

A son will always take after his father.
(Like father, like son.)
Yǒu qí fù bì yǒu qí zǐ.
有其父必有其子。

Good bamboo produces good bamboo shoots.

(Fine parents raise fine children.)

Hǎo zhú chū hǎo sǔn.

好竹出好笋。

A boatman's child knows how to stay afloat on the water.

(You can't help picking up something of your family's trade.)

Chuánjiā háizi huì fú shuǐ.

船家孩子会浮水。

The palm and the back of your hand are both your own flesh.

(Parents naturally feel equal love for all their children.)

Shǒu xīn shǒu bèi dōu shì ròu.

手心手背都是肉。

Other people's wives always seem better than your own; [but] your own children always seem better than other people's.

(In traditional China, you had no choice of a wife with arranged marriages, but every man has always favored his own children.)

Lǎopó shì biérén de hǎo, háizi shì zìjǐde hǎo.

老婆是别人的好，孩子是自己的好。

To give a child a thousand pieces of gold is not as good as giving him a skill.

Cì zǐ qiān jīn bù rú cì zǐ yí yì.

赐子千金不如赐子一艺。

船家孩子会浮水

A boatman's child knows how to stay afloat on the water

If you don't prune a tree, it won't become usable lumber; if you don't nurture a child, he won't become a true adult.
Shù bùxiū bùchéng cái, ér búyù bùchéng rén.
树不修不成材，儿不育不成人。

Children and grandchildren will enjoy their own blessings [when grown]; there is no need to labor like a draft animal to ensure their futures.
Ér sūn zì yǒu ér sūn fú, mò wèi ér sūn zuò mǎ niú.
儿孙自有儿孙福，莫为儿孙作马牛。

You have to run your own household to know the price of rice and firewood; you have to raise your own children to understand the sacrifices that parents make.
(It's only when we have children of our own that we come to understand how much is required of parents.)
Dāng jiā cái zhī chái mǐ guì; yǎng zǐ fāng xiǎo fù mǔ ēn.
当家才知柴米贵；养子方晓父母恩。

If the son is filial, his father's heart can rest easy.
Zǐ xiào fù xīn kuān.
子孝父心宽。

Of the myriad sins, lewdness heads the list; of the many virtues, filial piety is the first.

Wàn è fú wéi shǒu, bǎi shàn xiào wéi xiān.

万恶浮为首，百善孝为先。

There are three types of unfilial behavior, the greatest of which is to have no descendants.

(The Confucian philosopher Mencius stated in the fourth century BCE that the three major offenses against one's parents were not to give them grandsons, not to support them when alive, and not to give them a decent burial after they died.)

Búxiào yǒu sān, wú hòu wéi dà.

不孝有三，无后为大。

In the Yangtze River, the waves in back push forward the waves in front of them; each generation is even better than the previous one.

(The older generation helps the younger, stronger one on its way and is replaced by it in an endless cycle.)

Chángjiāng hòu làng cuī qián làng; yídài gèng bǐ yídài qiáng.

长江后浪催前浪；一代更比一代强。

HUSBAND AND WIFE

One day together as husband and wife is like a hundred days of grace.

(The marriage relationship is a true blessing.)

Yírì fūqī bǎirì ēn.

一日夫妻百日恩。

One day together as husband and wife is like a hundred days of grace
一日夫妻百日恩

Anger between husband and wife should not last the night.
(Couples should never go to bed angry.)
Fūqī wú gé xiǔ zhī chóu.
夫妻无隔宿之仇。

An amicable divorce is as important as an amicable marriage.
Hǎo hé hǎo sàn.
好合好散。

The husband of a virtuous wife seldom suffers misfortune.
Qī xián fū huò shǎo.
妻贤夫祸少。

A room full of sons and daughter cannot equal (the value of) a husband and wife who share a mat (on which to sit).
(A good marriage is worth more than any number of children.)
Mǎn táng ér nǚ dāngbùdé bànxí fūqī.
满堂儿女当不得半席夫妻。

It is preferable to tear down ten temples than to destroy one marriage.
(As sacrilegious as it would be to destroy a Buddhist temple, it is even more unpardonable to break up a marriage.)
Nìng chāi shí zuò miào, búpò yìmén hūn.
宁拆十座庙，不破一门婚。

A man who has no wife has no peace in his heart.
Nán ér wú qī xīn wú zhǔ.
男儿无妻心无主。

Even a thousand miles apart, a couple destined for one another are pulled together by an [invisible] thread.
(The traditional Chinese belief is that an old man in the moon will tie an invisible red thread to both a young man and a young woman who are destined to meet and marry, even if they were born far apart from one another.)
Qiān lǐ yīn yuán yí xiàn qiān.
千里姻缘一线牵。

If you are fated for one another, you will meet though separated by a thousand miles; if you are not fated for one another, you will not encounter each other even when face to face.
Yǒu yuán qiān lǐ lái xiāng huì, wú yuán duì miàn bù xiāng féng.
有缘千里来相会，无缘对面不相逢。

Binding two people together does not make them husband and wife.
(You can't force people to fall in love with one another.)
Kùnbǎng bùchéng fūqī.
捆绑不成夫妻。

A clever woman must often sleep next to a foolish man.
(A woman with brains often ends up married to a stupid man.)
Qiǎo fù cháng bàn zhuō fū mián.
巧妇常伴拙夫眠。

Even a tough man can't avoid [feeling] the wind by his pillow.
(Even the strongest man is necessarily influenced by his wife, so never make an enemy of a powerful man's spouse.)
Yìng hàn nán bì zhěn biān fēng.
硬汉难避枕边风。

Even a hero has trouble crossing the mountain pass of a beautiful woman.
(A true hero may be able to fight his way through a ravine held by enemy troops but will succumb to the power of a beautiful woman; rare is the man who will not be seduced by beauty.)
Yīngxióng nán guò měirén guān.
英雄难过美人关。

A husband and wife are actually birds from the same woods, but when the end comes each flies away on its own.
(Originally meant that no matter how close a husband and wife may be, when the end of life comes, they must go their own way. However, it is now used exclusively to mean that in spite of the closeness between a couple, if real trouble comes, they may try to save only themselves.)
Fūqī běn shì tóng lín niǎo; dà xiàn dàolái gèzì fēi.
夫妻本是同林鸟，大限到来各自飞。

12 Women

In traditional Chinese culture, as in almost every traditional culture, the position of women was subordinate to that of men. Women were taught to submit, first to their fathers, then to their husbands, and finally to their sons. They received no formal education and could not own property. Their only hope of achieving a position of respect was to marry and to live long enough to become the respected matriarch of their family. Although several women in Chinese history rose to become the effective rulers of the country, including the Empress Wu in the late seventh century and the Empress Dowager Ci Xi at the end of the nineteenth century, women were deemed inferior to men and treated accordingly.

The number of characters in the Chinese language that incorporate the pictograph for "woman" reveal much about how women were viewed in Chinese society. Among these characters are the words for "yielding," "jealousy," and "vanity." The character for "peace" shows a woman under a roof, with the implication that a woman's place was in the home. In part to limit their movement and ensure that they would remain in the home, women were subject to the tradition of having their feet broken

妇女能顶半边天

Women can hold up half the sky

and then bound, giving them feet that were permanently petite, which was considered attractive to men. By the early twentieth century, approximately half of all Chinese women had bound feet, which gave them a swaying effect when they moved.

All of this changed dramatically when the Chinese Communist Party came to power in 1949. One of the main tenets of the Chinese Communist Party was the equality of women, whose improved status was included in the constitution of 1954. Girls were to be granted educational opportunities equal to those of boys, and women were given the same property rights as men. According to Mao Zedong, women were to "hold up half the sky," working equally alongside men. Indeed, many women rose to positions of power within the government. In contemporary China more than half the doctors are female, and there is no profession that is not open to women. Yet in the countryside, where over half the Chinese population still lives, boys continue to be preferred to girls, just as in traditional times. A farmer's sons who can work alongside him in the fields are seen as his security in old age. The "one-child policy" has always allowed rural families to have a second child in an effort to have a son if their first child is a girl.

Almost all the sayings below are ancient ones that reflect the traditional view of women. Only the last is the slogan that

Mao Zedong was fond of quoting, which signaled a sea-change in the position of women in China.

Three women [together] make for a lively comedy (lit. folk opera).
(Whenever a group of women gather, there's bound to be a lot of lively talk.)
Sānge nǔrén yìtái xì.
三个女人一台戏。

A girl changes 18 times before becoming a woman.
(A girl changes so quickly and dramatically as she grows up that it seems as if she goes through myriad transformations; often said to assure parents that a girl going through an awkward age may end up a pretty woman.)
Nǔ dà shíbā biàn.
女大十八变。

A girl, once grown, cannot be kept at home.
(When a girl reaches marriageable age, she should be married, or trouble will be sure to follow.)
Nǔ dà bú zhòng liú.
女人不中留。

A daughter once married is like water spilled on the ground.
(After a daughter marries, she is lost to her family forever, because by tradition she goes to live with her husband's family.)
Jiàchūqù de nǔér, pōchūqù de shuǐ.
嫁出去的女儿，泼出去的水。

Women may be long on hair, but they're short on knowledge.
Nǚrén tóufa cháng, jiànshi duǎn.
女人头发长见识短。

A wise man does not argue with women.
(This is not because women know better than he does, but because women are so unreasonable that it is demeaning and pointless to argue with them!)
Hǎo nán bù gēn nǚ dòu.
好男不跟女斗。

An ugly woman must still meet her in-laws.
(No matter how unpleasant, some things just have to be done; sooner or later, you have to face the music.)
Chǒu xífù zǒngshì yào jiàn gōng pó de.
丑媳妇总是要见公婆的。

Men should fear entering the wrong profession; women should fear marrying the wrong man.
(For men, the way to advancement was through their work; for women, there was only marriage.)
Nán pà rù cuò háng, nǚ pà jià cuò láng.
男怕入错行，女怕嫁错郎。

Women can hold up half the sky.
(Women are capable of doing anything that men can do and have a responsibility to do their share. This was a Communist slogan quoted often by Mao Zedong.)
Fùnǚ néng dǐng bàn biān tiān.
妇女能顶半边天。

Fate

The Chinese have always been among the most fatalistic of people. In the West, we often say that our fate is determined by the will of God, but at the same time we also claim that we are "captains of our own ship, masters of our own destiny." Neither concept is reflected in the way that most Chinese view the world. Instead, the Chinese over time have expressed their sense that whatever man proposes, fate disposes. All is in the hands not of a loving God but of an indifferent fate or destiny. One of the most common expressions in contemporary Chinese when trying to find a solution to one of life's problems is *méiyǒu bànfǎ* (没有办法; there's nothing you can do about it).

Just as it is impossible for human beings to know what fate has in store or to change their "luck," it has always been considered equally impossible to challenge authority, whether political or within the family.

We have therefore included some famous proverbs about the futility of trying to stand up to the powers that be, as well as the impossibility of forestalling destiny.

One of the most famous proverbs is "The old man on the border loses his horse; who knows if it isn't good fortune [in

Everything is controlled by fate and not in the slightest by people

万事皆由命，半点不由人

disguise]." Often this is all that is recited, because all Chinese know the rest of the proverb: "The old man on the border gains a horse; who knows if it isn't misfortune (in disguise)." Equivalent English expressions include "Every cloud has a silver lining" and "It might be a blessing in disguise," by which we mean that when something unfortunate happens, it might turn out to be for the best. While the Chinese proverb acknowledges that, it also maintains that when something seemingly advantageous happens, it might turn out to be harmful in the end.

Like all four-character idioms, this saying is based on an ancient tale, in this case that of an old peasant whose home is close to the border with Mongolia. One day, his only horse, upon which he depends for plowing, runs away. When his neighbors all come to commiserate with him, he philosophically tells them that it might turn out to be for the best. Sure enough, several days later his horse returns, with a wild Mongolian pony trailing behind him. When all the neighbors come to congratulate the old man on this piece of unexpected good luck, the old man calmly philosophizes that this might turn out to be unfortunate in the end. As luck would have it, when the old man's only son tries to break in the wild pony by riding it, he falls from the horse and breaks his leg. The old man shrugs off the sympathy from his neighbors by maintaining that perhaps it might turn out to be good fortune. He's proven right when, days later, the army comes to the village to conscript young men to fight in faraway wars, with little likelihood that they will return. But because the old man's son has a broken leg, he is spared.

No other story better sums up the resignation to fate that most Chinese feel as well as their sense of powerlessness before forces greater than themselves.

THE FUTILITY OF FIGHTING FATE

Everything is controlled by fate and not in the slightest by people.

Wànshì jiē yóu mìng, bàn diǎn bù yóu rén.

万事皆由命，半点不由人。

If you have good luck, there is no misfortune to fear; if you have bad luck, there's no way to escape it.

Shì fú búshì huò, shì huò duǒbúguò.

是福不是祸，是祸躲不过。

The wind may arise and the clouds appear in the sky without warning; people's fortunes may change between dawn and dusk of the same day.

(Like the weather, one's fortune may change for better or worse at any time.)

Tiān yǒu bú cè fēng yún, rén yǒu dàn xī huò fú.

天有不测风云，人有旦夕祸福。

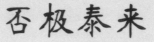

否极泰来

Good fortune may come out of the depths of misfortune

The heavens will rain, and women will want to marry.
(Many things in life are unavoidable, like rain and women desiring a husband, not to mention death and taxes!)
Tiān yào xiàyǔ, niáng yào jià rén.
天要下雨，娘要嫁人。

Blessings never come in pairs, but misfortunes never come singly.
Fú wú shuāng zhì, huò bù dān xíng.
福无双至，祸不单行。

Just when you have a leaky roof, you'll meet with a prolonged rain storm; just when your boat needs repairs, you'll meet with a head wind.
(When it rains, it pours; bad luck seems to strike us at the worst possible time.)
Wū lòu piān féng lián yīn yǔ; chuán pò piān yù dǐng tóu fēng.
屋漏偏逢连阴雨；船破偏遇顶头风。

Things don't go as we'd like 80–90% of the time.
Bù rúyì shì cháng bā jiǔ.
不如意事常八九。

CHALLENGING AUTHORITY AS FUTILE AS FIGHTING FATE

Like a praying mantis trying to block a chariot with its little arms
(You can't fight City Hall; it's useless for the "common man" to challenge the powers that be. This four-character idiom is based on the ancient fable of a praying mantis who felt himself so powerful that he tried to stand in the way of the king's chariot when it was about to pass by. While the king was impressed with the courage of the tiny insect, he was also amused that so small a creature thought he could block a horse-drawn chariot going full speed.)
Táng bì dǎng chē.
螳臂挡车

An ant who tries to topple a giant tree is laughable in his inability to know himself.
(Don't bite off more than you can chew; a man should know his limitations.)
Pí fú hàn dà shù, kě xiào bú zì liàng.
蚍蜉撼大树，可笑不自量。

EVERY CLOUD MAY HAVE A SILVER LINING (BUT EVERY CLEAR SKY MAY SOON HAVE CLOUDS!)

The old man on the border loses a horse; who knows if it isn't good fortune [in disguise]?
(The old man on the border gains a horse; who knows if it isn't bad fortune?)
Sài wēng shī mǎ, yān zhī fēi fú?
塞翁失马，焉知非福？

Heaven creates no paths that are completely impassible

天无绝人之路

Good fortune may come out of the depths of misfortune.
(Calm follows a storm.)
Pǐ jí tài lái.
否极泰来。

Purposely plant flowers, and the flowers won't necessarily blossom; mindlessly stick a willow sapling in the ground, and it may grow to give you shade.
(The best-laid plans of mice and men often go awry; we sometimes fail when trying too hard, but sometimes we succeed with very little effort.)
Yǒu yì zhòng huā huā bù fā, wú xīn chā liǔ liǔ chéng yīn.
有意种花花不发，无心插柳柳成荫。

Where the mountains end and the rivers peter out and you despair of ever finding the way, there beyond the dark willows and bright flowers lies another village.
(In the darkest hour, when things seem bleakest, you may spy light at the end of the tunnel.)
Shān qióng shuǐ jìn yí wú lù, liǔ àn huā míng yòu yì cūn.
山穷水尽疑无路，柳暗花明又一村。

NOT EVERY MISFORTUNE CAN BE BLAMED ON FATE. TOO OFTEN WE BRING MISFORTUNE DOWN ON OURSELVES.

Even when there are no problems out there [in the world], foolish people create trouble for themselves.
(Leave well enough alone; don't create problems where there aren't any.)
Tiānxià běn wú shì, yōng rén zì rǎo zhī.
天下本无事，庸人自扰之。

If at home you do not act morally, you'll encounter a storm when you go out your door.
(If in our daily lives we do immoral things, we'll eventually meet with disaster out in the world.)
Zài jiā bù xíng shàn, chū mén dà yǔ lín.
在家不行善，出门大雨淋。

BUT PERHAPS "WHERE THERE'S A WILL, THERE'S A WAY."

When your cart comes to a mountain, there's always a way [around it].
Chē dào shān qián bì yǒu lù.
车到山前必有路。

Heaven creates no paths that are completely impassible.
(When God closes a door, he opens a window.)
Tiān wú jué rén zhī lù.
天无绝人之路。

If it's not light in the east, then it's light in the west; if it's dark to the south, there's always the north.

(No matter how bleak things may look at any particular place and time, there is always the chance of better days ahead.)

Dōngfāng búliàng xīfāng liàng; hēile nánfāng yǒu běifāng.

东方不亮西方亮；黑了南方有北方。

Dark clouds can't blot out the sun.

Wū yún zhēbuzhù tàiyáng.

乌云遮不住太阳。

14 Animal Metaphors

Every culture has used animals in parables and metaphors to describe the range of human flaws and foibles, on the assumption that people are much more likely to accept criticism if it is made indirectly and humorously through animal, rather than human, figures. Because different cultures see a particular animal as representing a certain human virtue or vice, the use of animal imagery also allows for more colorful commentary on the human condition.

The English language, too, is full of proverbs that use examples from the animal world to cast light on the world of human beings. It has expressions like "You can't teach an old dog new tricks," "Curiosity killed the cat," "A leopard can't change its spots," "Birds of a feather flock together," and so on—to the point that most of the animal kingdom has been used metaphorically.

The Chinese language is especially rich with sayings that refer to animals. Some animals, like the tiger or the mythological dragon and phoenix, represent noble or heroic qualities. Other animals, including the snake, the rat, and the fox, embody the evil side of human nature. Still others, such as the horse, the ox, or the sheep, are symbolic of ordinary people.

What's interesting here is that, although most cultures in the world view the snake as evil, the fox as wily, and the ox as docile, other animals are viewed rather differently from one culture to another. The dragon, for instance, was viewed in the West as an evil monster that threatened human beings and should be killed. In China, however, the dragon represented the force of nature that controlled the sky and the life-giving rain. It was neither good nor bad, but rather the embodiment of a powerful natural phenomenon. The emperor of China was for centuries the only person in the kingdom allowed to wear robes embroidered with dragons or to have his walls adorned with them, including the famous Nine-Dragon Gate in the Forbidden City, the emperor's palace in Beijing.

For dog lovers, it is painful to note that, while the dog was usually portrayed as a rather lowly creature in English-language proverbs, in countless Chinese proverbs it is referred to as representative of the basest of people. In traditional China, most people were so poor that they had to struggle to feed themselves and could not afford to keep a dog. Only the rich landlord class raised dogs, which they kept not as pets but as guard dogs. These dogs would often chase and bite common people when they passed by, so they hated dogs because of what they represented.

English has sayings like "He who lies down with dogs gets fleas" and "Let sleeping dogs lie," with the latter advice implying that when the dogs awakes, it might attack you. When someone has sunk really low in life, it is said that he has "gone to the dogs." But it is also said that "Every dog has its day," and the dog is called "man's best friend."

The dog comes in for much rougher treatment in Chinese sayings, similar to how the pigs are referred to in English-language expressions. During the height of the Cultural Revolution

(1966–76), when the Chinese Communist government attacked capitalists (instead of embracing them, as it does now), it called them "running dogs" rather than the Western "capitalist pigs." Instead of the English-language expression "You can't make a silk purse out of a sow's ear," the Chinese say, "No ivory can come out of a dog's mouth." And when English speakers want to caution that a bad person is not likely to change, they say, "A leopard can't change its spots," whereas the Chinese will state: "A dog can't change his instinct to eat poop."

In contemporary China, at least in the cities, a great many Chinese now can keep dogs as pets and treat them as beloved members of the family, just as in the West.

ANIMALS THAT REPRESENT POWERFUL OR SUPERIOR PEOPLE

Tigers

If you don't enter the tiger's den, how will you ever get the tiger's cubs?
(Nothing ventured, nothing gained; No pain, no gain.)
Búrù hǔ xué, yān dé hǔ zǐ?
不入虎穴，焉得虎子？

To be in the king's company is tantamount to being in the company of a tiger.
Bàn jūn rú bàn hǔ.
伴君如伴虎。

养虎自遗患

To raise a tiger is to bring trouble to yourself

It is in the deepest mountains that tigers and leopards hide; it is in turbulent times that heroes emerge.
Shēn shān cáng hǔ bào, luàn shì chū yīngxióng.
深山藏虎豹，乱世出英雄。

A tiger father will not beget a puppy.
(A brave or talented father is unlikely to have a cowardly or untalented son.)
Hǔ fù wú quǎnzǐ.
虎父无犬子。

The tigers of East Mountain are man-eaters, as are the tigers of West Mountain.
(Evil or cruel people are the same everywhere.)
Dōng shān de lǎohǔ chī rén, xī shān de lǎohǔ yě chī rén.
东山的老虎吃人，西山的老虎也吃人。

You may be able to draw [sketch] a tiger's skin, but it's much harder to draw its bones; you may know a person's face, but it's difficult to know his heart.
(Since it's difficult to really know what another person is really thinking, you can never trust somebody completely.)
Huà hǔ huà pí nán huà gǔ, zhī rén zhī miàn bùzhī xīn.
画虎画皮难画骨，知人知面不知心。

You try to draw a tiger but end up only drawing a dog.

(mocking someone who tries to imitate someone superior, but clumsily ends up falling laughably short)

Huà hǔ bùchéng fǎn lèi quǎn.

画虎不成反类犬。

A tiger's head with a snake's tail

(mocking someone or something that begins grandly but finishes poorly)

Hǔ tóu shé wěi

虎头蛇尾

Clearly knowing there are tigers on the mountain, yet still headed to the tiger mountain

(To continue on undeterred by the possible danger or difficulty ahead—said either in praise or in criticism)

Míng zhī shān yǒu hǔ, piān xiàng hǔ shān xíng

明知山有虎，偏向虎山行

Follow a tiger, and you'll go into the mountains; follow an eagle, and you'll fly into the sky.

(You will be influenced more and more by the company you keep.)

Gēn hǔ jìn shān, gēn yīng fēi tiān.

跟虎进山，跟鹰飞天。

Even the most vicious tiger won't devour its cubs.

(Even the worst person isn't likely to harm his own children.)

Hǔ dú bùshí zǐ.

虎毒不食子。

Even tigers sometimes doze/take a nap.
(Even wise men make mistakes; Japanese equivalent: "Even monkeys sometimes fall from trees.")
Lián lǎohǔ hái yǒu dǎdǔn de shíhou ne.
连老虎还有打盹的时候呢。

When two tigers tussle, one is bound to get injured.
(When two powerful people come into conflict with one another, at least one is bound to get seriously hurt.)
Liǎng hǔ xiāng zhēng, bì yǒu yì shāng.
两虎相争，必有一伤。

Two tigers can't remain on the same mountain together.
(Two strong personalities in the same place will ultimately clash.)
Yìshān bùnéng cún èr hǔ.
一山不能存二虎。

A tiger and a leopard each goes its own way.
(To each his own; let others do their own thing without interfering.)
Lǎohǔ jīnqiánbào, gè zǒu gè de dào.
老虎金钱豹,各走各的道。

A person may not intend to harm the tiger, but the tiger may be intent on harming you.
(You always have to be suspicious of another's intentions, however harmless your own may be.)
Rén wú hài hǔ xīn, hǔ yǒu shāng rén yì.
人无害虎心，虎有伤人意。

Letting your illness go untreated is [as dangerous as] raising a tiger.
Yǎng bìng rú yǎng hǔ.
养病如养虎。

To raise a tiger is to bring trouble to yourself.
(One must always consider the consequences of one's actions; appeasing a powerful person may cause you trouble later on.)
Yǎng hǔ zì yí huàn.
养虎自遗患。

[Beware of] a tiger with a smiling face.
(You can't trust a potentially dangerous person simply because he is smiling at you.)
Xiào miàn hǔ.
笑面虎。

Even a skinny tiger has an ambitious heart.
(A person may still harbor ambitions, even when old or weak.)
Hǔ shòu xióng xīn zài.
虎瘦雄心在。

Fear people who are of one mind [united by a common cause] as much as tigers gathered into a pack.
Rén pà qí xīn, hǔ pà chéng qún.
人怕齐心，虎怕成群。

A dragon begets nine kinds of offspring, and all of them are different

一龙生九种，种种有别

When people turn 50 [years old], they're like tigers descending the mountain.

(When people are at the height of their ability and with an imposing dignity and ease, they have reached a high plateau in life.)

Rén dào wǔshí hǎo bǐ xià shān hǔ.

人到五十好比下山虎。

Dragons

The dragon who swims in shallow water becomes the sport of shrimp; the tiger who descends to level ground may be bullied by dogs.

(A man who loses position or influence may find himself subjected to much indignity.)

Lóng yóu qiǎn shuǐ zāo xiā xì, hǔ luò píng yáng bèi quǎn qī.

龙游浅水遭虾戏，虎落平阳被犬欺。

A dragon begets a dragon; a phoenix begets a phoenix; and a mouse's offspring know how to dig a hole.

(A child with clever and intelligent parents will inevitably turn out better than the child with dull and stupid ones.)

Lóng shēng lóng , fèng shēng fèng, lǎoshǔ de érzi huì dǎ dòng.
龙生龙，凤生凤，老鼠的儿子会打洞。

A dragon begets nine kinds of offspring, and all of them are different.
(Even great men's children vary in talent and ability.)
Yì lóng shēng jiǔ zhǒng, zhǒngzhǒng yǒu bié.
一龙生九种，种种有别。

A dragon's eyes recognize pearls; a phoenix's eyes recognize gems; a cow's eyes only recognize green grass.
(Superior people discern what is truly fine and beautiful, while ordinary people only know what's commonplace and practical.)
Lóng yǎn shí zhū, fèng yǎn shí bǎo, niú yǎn shí qīngcǎo.
龙眼识珠，凤眼识宝，牛眼识青草。

To add pupils to the eyes of the dragon you're painting
(to add the finishing touch that brings a work of art to life; a crucial touch in an argument that drives home a point)
Huà lóng diǎn zhū
画龙点珠

Phoenixes

If there's no wutong tree, you'll never attract a phoenix.
(Without a strong incentive, you'll never get a superior person to join you; the fabled phoenix, the paragon of birds, is said to perch only on a wutong tree, sometimes called a parasol tree.)
Méiyǒu wútóng shù, yǐnbúdào fènghuáng lái.
没有梧桐树，引不到凤凰来。

老鸹窝里出凤凰

From a crow's nest, a phoenix may emerge

A phoenix won't enter a crow's nest.
(How can a common crow be a fit mate for a rare phoenix?
People from different social backgrounds make a poor match for
a marriage.)
Fènghuáng búrù wūyā wō.
凤凰不入乌鸦窝。

From a crow's nest, a phoenix may emerge.
(It's possible for exceptional people to come from an ordinary
family.)
Lǎoguā wōlǐ chū fènghuáng.
老鸹窝里出凤凰。

ANIMALS THAT REPRESENT ORDINARY PEOPLE

Horses

**A good horse will never turn around to graze in an old
pasture.**
(People will not generally return to their old lover or their former workplace after they have left.)

106

Hǎo mǎ bù chī huítóu cǎo.
好马不吃回头草。

A good horse does not accept two saddles.
(A virtuous woman never marries twice.)
Hǎo mǎ búbèi shuāng ān, hǎo nǚ bùgēng èr fū.
好马不鞴双鞍，好女不更二夫。

A long journey will prove the stamina of a horse; the passage of time will show a person's true heart.
(You can only truly judge a person's character by long association with them.)
Lù yáo zhī mǎ lì, rì jiǔ jiàn rén xīn.
路遥知马力，日久见人心。

People may have a slip of the hand; horses may lose their footing.
(Everyone makes mistakes; no one's perfect, not even a surefooted horse.)
Rén yǒu cuò shǒu, mǎ yǒu shī tí.
人有错手，马有失蹄。

A speedy horse doesn't need to be whipped to be urged on; a loud drum doesn't need to be struck with a heavy hammer.
(A word to the wise is sufficient.)
Kuài mǎ búyòng biān cuī, xiǎng gǔ búyòng zhòng chuí.
快马不用鞭催，响鼓不用重锤。

A donkey's lips do not fit a horse's mouth.
(to give an answer that is beside the point)
Lǘ chún duìbushàng mǎ zuǐ.
驴唇对不上马嘴。

If a horse isn't given hay in the evening, it won't become stout [and strong]; a person without ill-gotten wealth can't become rich.

Mǎ wú yè cǎo bùféi, rén wú héng cái búfù.

马无夜草不肥，人无横财不富。

A man on horseback cannot understand how hard it is for a person who has to run [someone "under the horse"]; a sated man cannot understand how a hungry man feels.

(People in comfortable circumstances cannot fully empathize with those much less fortunate.)

Mǎ shàng bùzhī mǎ xià kǔ, bǎo hàn bùzhī è hàn jī.

马上不知马下苦，饱汉不知饿汉饥。

You want your horse to run while not wanting it to eat grass [get nourishment].

(You want to have your cake and eat it, too.)

Yòu yào mǎer pǎo, yòu yào mǎer bùchī cǎo.

又要马儿跑，又要马儿不吃草。

When a man is poor, his ambition does not reach far; when a horse is skinny, its hair appears long.

(Poverty stifles ambition.)

Rén qióng zhì duǎn, mǎ shòu máo cháng.

人穷志短，马瘦毛长。

When a man is kind, people will cheat him; when a horse is gentle, people will ride him.

Rén shàn yǒu rén qī, mǎ shàn yǒu rén qí.

人善有人欺，马善有人骑。

When shooting at a man, first shoot his horse; when catching robbers, first catch their leader.

Shè rén xiān shè mǎ, qín zéi xiān qín wáng.

射人先射马，擒贼先擒王。

Clothes make the man just as a saddle [with adornments] makes the horse.

(Clothes make the man.)

Rén shì yīshang, mǎ shì ān.

人饰衣裳，马饰鞍。

After a word is spoken, even a team of four horses cannot catch up to it.

(A word once said as a promise or in anger is not easily forgotten; be careful what you say, because words cannot be taken back.)

Yìyán jì chū, sì mǎ nán zhuī.

一言即出，驷马难追。

When in a stable to buy a horse, take a good look at its mother.

(The family we come from determines to a large extent who we become.)

Cáotóu mǎi mǎ, kàn mǔzi.

槽头买马，看母子。

It takes three years to learn a horse's nature, but five years to know a person's heart.

Sān nián shí mǎ xìng, wǔ nián dǒng rén xīn.

三年识马性，五年懂人心。

When the horse is slow, we complain that the whip is used too lightly; when we're impatient, we complain that the cart is too slow.

(To an impatient person, time seems to pass too slowly.)

Mǎ chí xián biān qīng; xīn jí xián chē màn.

马迟嫌鞭轻；心急嫌车慢。

An old horse knows the way.

(Wisdom often comes with age.)

Lǎo mǎ shí tú.

老马识途。

A haggard [starving] camel is still bigger than a horse.

(A rich person fallen on hard times is still better off than ordinary working people.)

Shòusǐ de luòtuó bǐ mǎ dà.

瘦死的骆驼比马大。

Oxen

To eat a chestnut, you have to remove the shell; to lead an ox, you have to lead it by the nose.

(To solve any problem, you have to grasp the essential point.)

Chī lì yào bō pí, qiān niú yào qiān bí.

吃栗要剥皮，牵牛要牵鼻。

To forcibly lower a cow's head when it doesn't want to drink water

(To force somebody to do something against their will, which is bound to end in failure)

Niú bùchī shuǐ qiáng àn tóu

牛不吃水强按头

A newborn calf has no fear of tigers.
(Youth is fearless.)
Chūshēng niúdú búpà hǔ.
初生牛犊不怕虎。

To play the lute for cows
(Japanese: "To throw copper coins in front of a cat"; the Bible:
"Casting pearls before swine")
Duì niú tán qín
对牛弹琴

A gentleman never argues with an ox.
(The superior person does not try to argue with a base or stupid
person.)
Jūnzǐ bùgēn niú zhìqì.
君子不跟牛执气。

　　Pigs

People fear getting famous; pigs fear getting fat.
(Although fame is assumed as a blessing, it can bring trouble to
people, just as a pig getting fat seems a blessing because it's well
fed, but only hastens the day it ends up as bacon. See the same
proverb in Chapter 7, above, in a different context.)
Rén pà chū míng, zhū pà zhuàng.
人怕出名，猪怕壮。

**When there's no food in the trough, pigs will jostle one
another.**
(Shortage leads to internal conflict.)
Cáo nèi wú shí, zhū gǒng zhū.
槽内无食，猪拱猪。

狗嘴里吐不出象牙

No ivory can come out of a dog's mouth

Even if you've never eaten pork, surely, you've seen a pig run?
("Don't you know *anything*?!"—said teasingly.)
Nǐ méi chīguò zhūròu yě méi kànguò zhū pǎo ma?
你没吃过猪肉 也没看过猪跑吗？

A dead pig does not fear scalding water.
(criticizing someone for being shameless or describing the defiant attitude of someone who has nothing to lose)
Sǐ zhū búpà kāishuǐ tàng .
死猪不怕开水烫。

ANIMALS THAT REPRESENT BASE AND LOWLY PEOPLE

Dogs

Don't strike a dog until you see its master's face.
(Don't attack someone until you know whom he serves.)
Dǎ gǒu kàn zhǔ miàn.
打狗看主面。

A good dog doesn't get under foot.
(used in a derogatory way to criticize someone from blocking your way)
Hǎo gǒu búdǎng lù (dào).
好狗不挡路（道）。

A dog is superior to a chicken and so will never fight with a chicken; a good man will never fight with a woman.
(Since women are inferior to men in reasoning and therefore unreasonable, a man should never try to argue with a woman.)
Hǎo gǒu bù hé jī dòu, hǎo nán bù yǔ nǚ dòu.
好狗不和鸡斗，好男不与女斗。

No ivory can come out of a dog's mouth.
(A foul-mouthed or bad-intentioned person can't be expected to say anything decent; you can't make a silk purse out of a sow's ear.)
Gǒu zuǐlǐ tǔbùchū xiàngyá.
狗嘴里吐不出象牙。

A dog can't change his instinct to eat poop.
(Bad habits are hard to change; bad people don't change easily.)
Gǒu gǎibùliǎo chī shǐ.
狗改不了吃屎。

A wolf will walk a thousand miles and still eat people; a dog will go to the end of the earth and still eat garbage.
(Bad people never change their vicious ways.)
Láng zǒu qiān lǐ chī rén, gǒu dào tiān biān chī shǐ.
狼走千里吃人，狗到天边吃屎。

A rabbit when cornered will turn around and become fierce as a tiger

兔子回头凶似虎

A dog can only look at a person from down below.

(A low, base person sees everyone else as equally low.)

Gǒu yǎn kàn rén dī.

狗眼看人低。

When a person is desperate, he'll rebel and fight back; when a dog is desperate, it'll even leap over a wall.

(Don't push someone too far, or he'll take desperate measures.)

Rén jí zàofǎn, gǒu jí tiàoqiáng.

人急造反，狗急跳墙。

A mangy cur can't make it over a wall even when helped.

(You will achieve nothing by trying to help a worthless person.)

Lài gǒu fúbúshàng qiáng.

癞狗扶不上墙。

A golden nest or a silver nest cannot compare to one's own humble [dog's] nest.

(Be it ever so humble, there's no place like home.)

Jīn wō yín wō, bùrú zìjǐ de gǒu wō.

金窝银窝，不如自己的狗窝。

Fierce dogs bite people without showing their teeth.
(The most dangerous people are those who hide their evil intentions.)
È gǒu yǎo rén búlù yá.
恶狗咬人不露牙。

When one dog barks at a shadow, a hundred bark at the sound.
(People will mindlessly repeat what they hear in the way of gossip.)
Yìquǎn fèi xíng, bǎi quǎn fèi shēng.
一犬吠形，百犬吠声。

ANIMALS THAT REPRESENT MEEK PEOPLE

Rabbits/Hares

The wily hare has three holes to his burrow.
(A cunning person will have several aces up his sleeve.)
Jiǎo tù sān kū.
狡兔三窟。

Even rabbits will bite you if desperate enough.
(Be careful not to push somebody too far.)
Tùzi jíle yě yǎo rén.
兔子急了也咬人。

Rabbits never eat the grass that borders their burrow.
(Even a villain won't harm his neighbors.)
Tùzi bùchī wō biān cǎo.
兔子不吃窝边草。

A rabbit's tail can only grow so long.
(Nothing lasts very long, including an evil person's hold on power.)
Tùzi wěibā chángbùliǎo.
兔子尾巴长不了。

Don't let loose the falcon until you see the hare.
(Don't shoot until you see the whites of his eyes; don't give your enemy advance warning until you're ready to strike.)
Bújiàn tùzi bùsā yīng.
不见兔子不撒鹰。

A rabbit [when cornered] will turn around and become fierce as a tiger.
(When pushed too far, even the weak or meek will put up a fight.)
Tùzi huítóu xiōng sì hǔ.
兔子回头凶似虎。

A rabbit cannot be harnessed to [pull] a carriage.
(Never rely on an incapable person to shoulder heavy responsibilities beyond his/her ability.)
Tùzi jiàbuliǎo yuán.
兔子驾不了辕。

Chickens

Why use a knife designed to butcher cattle to kill a chicken?
(Why swat a fly with a sledge hammer?)
Shā jī yān yòng niú dāo?
杀鸡焉用牛刀?

Kill a chicken to frighten the monkeys.
(Punish someone as an example to others.)
Shā jī gěi hóu kàn.
杀鸡给猴看。

Kill the hen to get the eggs.
(Kill the goose that lays the golden eggs.)
Shā jī qǔ luǎn.
杀鸡取卵。

If a person makes it in life, even his chickens and dogs are exalted.
(When someone rises to a position of fortune and fame, his followers will rise to success on his coattails.)
Yì rén dé dào, jī quǎn shēng tiān.
一人得道，鸡犬升天。

A [chicken] egg can't smash a rock.
(The weak have no chance to defeat the powerful.)
Jīdàn pèngbúguò shítóu.
鸡蛋碰不过石头。

ANIMALS THAT REPRESENT EVIL PEOPLE

Snakes

When striking/attacking a snake, first strike its head.
(In catching crooks, first catch their leader.)
Dǎ shé xiān dǎ tóu, qín zéi xiān qín wáng.
打蛇先打头，擒贼先擒王。

One grain of mouse droppings will ruin an entire pot of soup

一粒老鼠屎，坏了一锅汤

A person whose heart is not content is like a snake that tries to swallow an elephant.

(Discontent leads one to seek things beyond reason.)

Rén xīn bùzú shé tūn xiàng.

人心不足蛇吞象。

A snake cannot go anywhere when its head is gone; a bird cannot fly without its wings.

(Any army or gang ceases to be a threat if you can dispatch its leader.)

Shé wú tóu ér bùxíng, niǎo wú chì ér bùfēi.

蛇无头而不行，鸟无翅而不飞。

Once bitten by a snake in the morning, a person will fear the rope at the well for the next three years.

(Once bitten, twice shy.)

Yídàn zāo shé yǎo, sān nián pà jǐng shéng

一旦遭蛇咬，三年怕井绳。

The mightiest dragon can't overcome the chief snake of the district.

(Even the most powerful person sometimes has to kowtow to the local strongman or bandit chief.)

Qiáng lóng yābúguò dì tóu shé.
强龙压不过地头蛇。

To add feet when painting a snake
(Don't gild the lily; quit while you're ahead; don't add anything to something that's already perfect. This four-character proverb is based on the ancient tale of a painting contest. Each contestant was to draw a snake. He who finished first would be declared the winner. One painter finished well ahead of the others. He decided that this gave him time to embellish his drawing by adding feet to the snake. He was then disqualified, because snakes have no feet!)
Huà shé tiān zú
画蛇添足

Mice and Rats

To be yelled at and beaten like a rat who runs across the street
(to be the object of universal condemnation)
Lǎoshǔ guòjiē, rénrén hǎn dǎ
老鼠过街，人人喊打

Like a mouse who encounters a cat
(to be fearful of someone)
Lǎoshǔ jiàndao māo
老鼠见到猫

Spare the rat to save the dish.
(to hold back from taking action against an evil-doer for fear of involving innocent people)
Tóu shǔ jì qì.
投鼠忌器。

One grain of mouse droppings will ruin an entire pot of soup.
(One rotten apple will spoil the whole barrel; one bad person or one careless act can ruin an entire enterprise.)
Yílì lǎoshǔ shǐ, huàile yìguō tāng.
一粒老鼠屎，坏了一锅汤。

A mouse will bravely shoulder a rifle in its own nest.
(poking fun at someone who's a tiger at home or in his own little bailiwick, but timid out in the world)
Hàozi káng qiāng wō lǐ hèng.
耗子扛枪窝里横。

A mouse can only see one inch in front of its nose.
(Small-minded people lack a broad view of things.)
Shǔ mù cùn guāng.
鼠目寸光。

Foxes and Weasels

A fox can never hide his tail.
(One's true character/evil intentions will eventually be revealed.)
Húlǐde wěibā zǒngshì cángbuzhù de.
狐狸的 尾巴总是藏不住的。

A fox isn't aware its tail stinks.
(People often cannot see their own shortcomings.)
Húlǐ bùzhī wěibā chòu.
狐狸不知尾巴臭。

When a weasel comes to pay his respects to the chicken at the new year, he harbors no good intentions.
(Beware of Greeks bearing gifts; do not trust the smiling countenance of a known villain.)
Huángshǔláng gěi jī bài nián, bùhuái hǎo yì.
黄鼠狼给鸡拜年，不怀好意。

Cats

Cats who love to meow can't catch mice.
Hào jiào de māo dǎibùzhǎo lǎoshǔ.
好叫的猫逮不着老鼠。

It doesn't matter whether a cat is white or black, as long as it can catch mice [it's a good cat].
(The ends justify the means; this quote is attributed to Deng Xiaoping, leader of China in the 1980s, explaining why he had decided to adopt capitalism in a Communist state.)
Bái māo hēi māo, néng dǎi hàozi jiùshi hǎo māo.
白猫黑猫，能逮耗子就是好 猫。

Better to be a bird's head than a cow's rump

宁为鸡首，不为牛后

Where is there a cat who won't steal fish? OR Where is there a rat who won't steal oil?
(It's irrational to expect that people will never fail morally, given human weakness; often used in reaction to news of an extramarital affair.)
Nǎ yǒu māoer bùtōu xīng.
哪有猫儿不偷腥。

  OR

Nǎ yǒu hàozi bùtōu yóu.
哪有耗子不偷油。

A blind cat bumping into a dead rat
(to discover something by chance, through dumb luck)
Xiā māo zhuàngdào sǐ hàozi
瞎猫撞到死耗子

A victorious cat is like an overjoyed tiger.
(Our smallest achievements may make us feel like a hero.)
Dé shèng de māoér huān sì hǔ.
得胜的猫儿欢似虎。

OTHER ANIMALS

Wild Geese

When a man passes away, all he leaves behind is his reputation; when a wild goose passes by, all he leaves is his cry.
(A person's only legacy is his reputation.)
Rén guò liú míng, yàn guò liú shēng.
人过留名，雁过留声。

To pluck a feather from a passing wild goose
(to take advantage of the smallest opportunity that presents itself, if there's any benefit to be had)
Yàn guò bá máo
雁过拔毛

Wild geese fear being separated from the flock; people fear falling behind the group.
(People fear being without friends and family.)
Yàn pà lí qún, rén pà diào duì.
雁怕离群，人怕掉队。

Other Birds

All crows the world over are black.
(Bad people and corrupt officials everywhere are equally bad.)
Tiānxià lǎoyā yìbān hēi.
天下老鸦一般黑。

吃鱼先拿头

To catch fish to eat, first grab a hold of the head

A sparrow may be tiny, but it has both a liver and a spleen [all internal organs].
(often used to describe a workplace that may be small but has everything needed to function successfully)
Máquè suí xiǎo, gān dǎn jù quán.
麻雀虽小，肝胆俱全。

How can a swallow know the ambition of a swan?
(Ordinary people cannot understand the mind of a heroic person with great ambitions.)
Yàn què yān zhī hóng hú zhī zhì?
燕雀焉知鸿鹄之志？

When the snipe and the clam fight, it's the fisherman who profits.
(A house divided against itself cannot stand.)
Yù bàng xiāng zhēng, yú rén dé lì.
鹬蚌相争，渔人得利。

People die in pursuit of wealth; birds die in pursuit of food.
(Greed can lead to one's demise.)
Rén wèi cái sǐ, niǎo wèi shí wáng.
人为财死，鸟为食亡。

124

In a large wood, you'll find every kind of bird.
(It takes all kinds; in a large group of people, there are always some "turkeys.")
Línzi dà le shénme niǎoer dōu yǒu.
林子大了什么鸟儿都有。

Better to be a bird's head than a cow's rump.
(Better to be a big fish in a little pond than a little fish in a big pond.)
Nìng wéi jī shǒu, bù wéi niú hòu.
宁为鸡首，不为牛后。

Birds without a head can't fly; wild beasts without a head can't walk.
(Any group of villains is powerless without a leader.)
Niǎo wú tóu bù fēi, shòu wú tóu bù zǒu.
鸟无头不飞，兽无头不走。

Fish

Big fish eat little fish; small fish eat little shrimp.
(The strong bully the weak; it's a "dog-eat-dog world.")
Dà yú chī xiǎo yú, xiǎo yú chī xiamǐ.
大鱼吃小鱼，小鱼吃虾米。

To catch a big fish, one must cast a long line.
(To get something big, you have to have a long-term plan.)
Fàng cháng xiàn diào dà yú.
放长线钓大鱼。

苍蝇不抱没缝的蛋

No fly will latch onto uncracked eggs

One mudfish can't stir up big waves.
(said of someone too insignificant to make trouble)
Yìtiáo níqiū fānbùqǐ dà làng.
一条泥鳅翻不起大浪。

If water is too clear [and pure], you can't raise fish.
(You can't be too trivial or too inflexible about small matters.
Compromise is often required to get what you want.)
Shuǐ qīng bùyǎng yú.
水清不养鱼。

Big fish can't be raised in a shallow pond.
(Talented people won't stay in a place that doesn't allow them
to use their talents fully.)
Chí qiǎn bùnéng yǎng dà yú.
池浅不能养大鱼。

To catch fish to eat, first grab a hold of the head.
(To catch a gang of thieves, first capture the leader.)
Chī yú xiān ná tóu.
吃鱼先拿头。

He who rides a donkey knows not the suffering of the person leading the donkey on foot.

(People who are well off seldom are aware of the hardships of the less fortunate.)

Qí lǘ bùzhī gǎn jiǎo de kǔ.

骑驴不知赶脚的苦。

If you're not willing to part with your child [temporarily, as bait], you'll never lure the wolf into your trap.

(One has to be willing to make a sacrifice to accomplish something important.)

Shèbùdé háizi tàobúzhù láng.

舍不得孩子套不住狼。

When the tree falls, the monkeys will scatter.

(When an influential person falls from power, his hangers-on disperse.)

Shù dǎo húsūn sàn.

树倒猢狲散。

A sheep's wool must be taken off the sheep's body.

(Ultimately you have to pay for whatever you get; nothing is really free.)

Yángmáo chū zài yáng shēnshàng.

羊毛出在羊身上。

Fasten the gate after the sheep have already been lost.

(Too little, too late; close the gate after the horse has bolted; an ounce of prevention is worth a pound of cure.)

Wáng yáng bǔ láo.

亡羊补牢。

Like two grasshoppers tied by the same thread

(said of two people inextricably bound together in an enterprise, so that one cannot get out of it without the other)

Yī gēn xiàn shàng shuànzhe liǎngge màzha

一根线上拴着两个蚂蚱

Each crab is smaller than the one before.

(often used to lament that a new official is even worse than the one he replaced)

Yíxiè bùrú yíxiè.

一蟹不如一蟹。

No fly will latch onto uncracked eggs.

(Evil people only gather round to corrupt those who have weaknesses.)

Cāngyīng búbào méi fèng de dàn.

苍蝇不抱没缝的蛋。

Like blind men touching an elephant [from the Buddhist scriptures]

(Truth is relative and subjective; each of us is like a sightless person who blindly comes into contact with but one part of the elephant and assume that from that one small part we can know the whole.)

Xiāzi mō xiàng

瞎子摸象

15 Food

Food plays an important role in every culture. After all, human beings need food to live. Moreover, eating is a great pleasure as well as a necessity, so it's no wonder that people have always been obsessed with food. Perhaps no other culture in the world, however, is quite as focused on food as are the Chinese. What other major language says "hello" by asking "Have you eaten?" (*Nǐ chīle ma?* 你吃了吗？). Because in ancient times most ordinary Chinese people did not have the means to ensure that they always had enough to eat, the assumption was that if you were fortunate enough to have eaten, you must be faring well in general. And what other culture expresses the sense that it takes time to accomplish great things not by referring to how long it took to construct Rome but, rather, by stating: "A fat person didn't get fat with just one bite" (*Pàngzi búshì yìkǒu chī de* 胖子不是一口吃的)?

The English language has a great many expressions that use food analogies. A person in a position of power is called a "big cheese" or a "big tomato." We all want to get "a piece of the pie" and to "bring home the bacon." Compared with Chinese, however, the number of proverbs that employ references to food or

Dishes without salt are tasteless; words without reason are powerless

菜没盐，无味；话没理，无力

eating—such as "Don't bite off more than you can chew," "Cream will rise to the top," and "You'll get your just desserts"—is more limited.

Chinese has a smorgasbord of sayings and expressions related to food and with eating. We start with a taste of the most famous proverbs related to food before moving on to dessert with some of the lesser-known ones.

PROVERBS

The people are the foundation of the country, and food is of the highest importance to the people.
Guó yǐ mín wéi běn, mín yǐ shí wéi tiān.
国以民为本，民以食为天。 —*Lao Zi*

If man is iron, food is steel.
(As strong as people may be, they'll collapse for certain without food. Iron is strong, but ultimately capable of being bent; not so with steel, which is unbendable—hence the metaphor for food being indispensable for human existence.)

Rén shì tiě, fàn shì gāng.
人是铁，饭是钢。

A fat person didn't get fat with just one mouthful.
(Rome wasn't built in a day.)
Pàngzi búshì yìkǒu chīde.
胖子不是一口吃的。

If you wish to be an extraordinary person, you have to taste the bitterest of the bitter.
Chīde kǔzhōngkǔ, fāngwéi rénshàngrén.
吃得苦中苦，方为人上人。

Food and clothing won't eat up your fortune, but lack of planning will.
(You can't eat yourself into poverty and you can't become poor by buying clothes, [but if] your planning is not thorough, you'll become poor during your lifetime.)
Chībùqióng, chuānbùqióng, suànjì búdào yíshì qióng.
吃不穷，穿不穷，算计不到一世穷。

If you sit and eat [all the time], even a mountain [of wealth] can be emptied.
(Idleness will lead you to eat up all your wealth.)
Zuò chī shān kōng.
坐吃山空。

To eat fish but complain of the fishy taste
(to have illogical expectations; not to see the obvious)
Chī yú yòu xián xīng
吃鱼又嫌腥

天下没有不散的宴席

There is no banquet that doesn't eventually break up

[Even] a clever woman cannot cook a meal without rice.
(You can't make bricks without straw; you can't make a silk
purse out of a sow's ear.)
Qiǎo fù nán wéi wú mǐ zhī chuī.
巧妇难为无米之炊。

**People will eat/accept softness when they'll refuse to eat/
accept hardness.**
(You can catch more flies with honey than with vinegar.)
Chī ruǎn bù chī yìng.
吃软不吃硬。

**[If] you have accepted a meal from someone, your tongue
is softened; if you accept gifts from someone, your arms'
reach is shortened.**
(Once you have accepted bribes from someone, you don't dare
criticize them or punish them if they do anything wrong.)
Chīle rénjiā de zuǐ ruǎn, ná rénjiā de shǒu duǎn.
吃人家的嘴软，拿人家的手软。

**You can't tell whether or not a stuffed bun has meat inside
just from looking at the outside.**
[lit., the outer folds of dough or "skin"]

(You can't judge a book by its cover—although the Chinese mainly use this to describe affluent people who do not flaunt their wealth.)

Bāozi yǒu ròu, búzài zhě shàng.

包子有肉，不在褶上。

Neither eat things haphazardly nor gossip haphazardly.

(Be careful about what you say as well as about what you eat.)

Dōngxī bùkě luàn chī, xiánhuà bùkě luàn jiǎng.

东西不可乱吃，闲话不可乱讲。

An [unripe] melon torn from the vine isn't sweet.

(Anything you do forcibly is not going to end well; the time must be right.)

Qiáng niǔ de gua ér bùtián.

强扭的瓜儿不甜。

A hundred people have a hundred different tastes [in food].

(Different strokes for different folks.)

Bǎi rén chī bǎi wèi.

百人吃百味。

A hundred kinds of rice feed a hundred kinds of people.

(People are all different in their personalities.)

Bǎi yàng mǐ yǎng bǎi yàng rén.

百样米养百样人。

Dishes without salt are tasteless; words without reason are powerless.

(If you speak irrationally, you will most likely persuade no one.)

Cài méi yán, wú wèi; huà méi lǐ, wú lì.

菜没盐，无味；话没理，无力。

When your belly is empty, you can't wait for the early rice to turn yellow [ripen].

(Promises for the future are of no help to a desperate person.)

È dùzi děngbùdé zǎodào huáng.

饿肚子等不得早稻黄。

One who is starving is not picky about food.

[One who is freezing is not picky about clothing; one who is lost is not picky about the road he takes; one who is poor is not picky about a wife.]

(Beggars can't be choosers; when someone is in dire straits, he or she will often settle for a poor choice.)

Jī bù zé shí, hán bù zé yī, huāng bù zé lù, pín bù zé qī.

饥不择食，寒不择衣，慌不择路，贫不择妻。

When eating, take care not to choke; when walking, take care you don't fall.

Chīfàn fáng yē, zǒu lù fáng diē.

吃饭防噎，走路防跌。

The raw rice has already been cooked.

(The die has already been cast; what's done cannot be undone.)

Shēng mǐ chéngle shú fàn.

生米成了熟饭。

Until the cooking is done, don't lift the lid off the wok.

(Wait to take action until the time is right.)

Búdào huǒ hòu bùjiē guō.

不到火候不揭锅。

Eat a full breakfast, eat a good lunch, but only eat a small supper.
(Eat breakfast like a king, lunch like a prince, but dinner like a pauper.)
Zǎofàn chī de bǎo, zhōngfàn chī de hǎo, wǎnfàn chī de shǎo.
早饭吃得饱，中饭吃得好，晚饭吃得少。

Governing a large nation is like cooking a small fish.
(If you gut it or scale it, too much handling will spoil it.)
Zhì dà guó rú pēng xiǎo yú.
治大国如烹小鱼。 —*Lao Zi*

There is no banquet that doesn't eventually break up.
(All good things come to an end; nothing lasts forever.)
Tiānxià méiyǒu búsàn de yānxí.
天下没有不散的宴席。

EXPRESSIONS RELATED TO FOOD

Hello
(Have you eaten?)
Nǐ chīle ma?
你吃了吗？

To suffer
(to eat bitterness)
chīkǔ
吃苦

Eat a full breakfast, eat a good lunch, but only eat a small supper

早饭吃得饱，中饭吃得好，晚饭吃得少

To suffer misfortune
(to eat misfortune)
chīkuī
吃亏

To be surprised/alarmed
(to eat surprise)
chījīng
吃惊

That's a shame; that's too bad
(spoiled cake)
Zāogāo!
糟糕

Cheese!, i.e., Smile!
(Eggplant!)
Qiézi!
茄子

Sour grapes
(Grapes that we can't eat we call sour.)
Chībúdào de pútáo shì suānde.
吃不到的葡萄是酸的

To flirt with women

(to eat tofu)

Chī dòufŭ.

吃豆腐

An ugly (or inferior) man wanted to marry a young, pretty woman.

(The toad wanted to eat the swan's flesh.)

Làihāma xiǎng chī tiāné ròu.

癞蛤蟆想吃天鹅肉。

A country bumpkin

(a potato)

tǔdòu

土豆

Dummy; silly guy

(dumb melon)

shǎyuā

傻瓜

Camera for dummies, i.e., easy-to-use camera

("dumb melon" camera)

shǎguā zhàoxiàngjī

傻瓜照相机

Idiot! Dummy!

(stupid egg)

bèndàn

笨蛋

人是铁，饭是钢

If man is iron, food is steel

To tantalize
(to make one's mouth water)
diàorén wèikǒu
吊人胃口

A job for life; the livelihood you depend on
(an iron rice bowl)
tiě fànwǎn
铁饭碗

To receive the same pay whether one works hard or not
(to eat from the same big pot)
chī dà guō fàn
吃大锅饭

To sponge off someone
(to eat rice without giving anything in return)
chī báishí
吃白食

To do something senselessly
(to be restless from overeating)
chī bǎole chēngde
吃饱了撑的

To be looked on with contempt; to be looked down upon
(to eat/suffer the whites of other people's eyes)
chī báiyǎn
吃白眼

To be denied entrance at the door; to be refused admission as an unwelcome guest
(to eat closed-door gruel)
chī bìmén gēng
吃闭门羹

To refuse to share with others
(to eat solitary food)
chī dú shí
吃独食

To get slapped on the face; to have one's ears boxed
(to eat/suffer ear burning)
chī ěrguāng
吃耳光

To eke out a living as a lowly paid teacher
(to eat chalk dust)
chī fěnbǐ huī
吃粉笔灰

To receive a salary from the government
(to eat the grains of officialdom)
chī guān liáng
吃官粮

To get more than you bargained for; to bear the consequences
(carry away in a bag what you can't eat)
chībùliǎo dōuzhe zǒu
吃不了兜着走

To be sued in a court of law
(to eat/suffer an official lawsuit)
chī guānsi
吃官司

To cry over spilled milk
(to eat the medicine of regret)
chī hòuhuǐ yào
吃后悔药

To be hard-pressed; to be in a critical situation
(to eat tightness)
chī jǐn
吃紧

To put out a lot of effort; to be under a strain
(to eat effort)
chī jìn
吃劲

Requiring a lot of effort; strenuous
(to eat exertion)
chī lì
吃力

A thankless task; to be a fool for one's pains
(to eat effort but not ingratriate oneself)
chī lì bù tǎo hǎo
吃力不讨好

To live off one's past achievements or glory
(to eat one's old capital/principal, monetarily speaking)
chī lǎo běn
吃老本

To live off one person while secretly helping another
(to eat inside, but crawl outside)
chī lǐ pá wài
吃里爬外

To be paid in spite of not making much of an effort
(to eat grain without taking care of things)
chī liáng bù guǎn shì
吃粮不管事

To be in a bad mood and not amenable to reason; irritable
(to eat gun drugs)
chī qiāng yào
吃枪药

To be shot dead by a bullet
(to eat a gun)
chī qiāngzǐr
吃枪子儿

A fat person didn't get fat with just one mouthful

胖子不是一口吃的

To accept an invitation to dinner [usually in return for a favor granted]
(to eat an invitation)
chī qǐng
吃请

To have a thorough grasp/understanding of something
(to eat/bite clear through)
chī tòu
吃透

To lead an idle life; to be a loafer or sponger
(to eat the food of idleness)
chī xián fàn
吃闲饭
  OR
(to eat food already prepared)
chī xiànchéng fàn
吃现成饭

To be very popular; to be much sought after
(to eat fragrance)
chī xiāng
吃香

To live it up; to be in clover
(to eat the fragrant and drink the spicy)
chī xiāng de hē là de
吃香的喝辣的

To endure small losses for the sake of a big gain
(to eat/suffer a small misfortune to capture a big advantage)
chī xiǎo kuī zhàn dà piányi
吃小亏占大便宜

To be treated in a favored way; to enjoy some kind of privilege
(to eat from a small stove)
chī xiǎo zào
吃小灶

To be suspicious; overly sensitive
(to eat one's heart)
chī xīn
吃心

To fail an exam
(to eat a duck egg)
chī yādàn
吃鸭蛋

To be cheated but unable to speak out about it
(to eat/suffer a deaf-mute's misfortune)
chī yǎbā kuī
吃哑巴亏

强扭的瓜儿不甜

An unripe melon torn from the vine isn't sweet

To take medicine
(to eat medicine)
chī yào
吃药

To be forced to suffer in silence
(like a deaf-mute who has "eaten" bitter medicine but is unable
to speak out and complain)
Yǎbā chī huáng lián, yǒu kǔ shuōbùchū
哑巴吃黄连,有苦说不出

To be insatiably greedy; never satisfied
(to eat what's in the bowl while eyeing what's in the wok)
chīzhe wǎn lǐ qiáozhe guō lǐ
吃着碗里瞧着锅里

To take the blame
(to eat the sin/crime)
chī zuì
吃罪

To show no mercy; to treat people ruthlessly
(to devour someone without even spitting out the bones)

chī rén bù tǔ gǔtóu
吃人不吐骨头

To take advantage of others at every opportunity
(A big mouth eats everything in every direction.)
dà zuǐ chī shí fāng.
大嘴吃十方。

I can take it or leave it.
(If you eat it, it's tasteless, but it would be a shame to throw it away.)
shí zhī wúwèi, qì zhī kěxī.
食之无味，弃之可惜。

[Only] one radish per hole
(Each person has his own task and can't leave his/her work or post to help with someone else's work.)
Yígè luóbo, yígè kēng.
一个萝卜一个坑

Two bitter melons on the same vine
(two people who have suffered the same bitter experiences in life)
Yìtiáo téngshàng de liǎngge kǔguā
一条藤上的两个苦瓜

16

Miscellaneous Favorite Sayings

Below are some of the most popular sayings in China that do not fall easily into any of the categories in the preceding chapters. We would be remiss if we left out such commonly heard nuggets of wisdom, which are some of our favorites.

AN INDIVIDUAL'S POSITION IN SOCIETY

The emperor's daughter need not worry about [a lack of] suitors.
(When you're the best at what you do, people will always seek you out without your needing to go in search of clients or customers.)
Huángdì de nǚér bùchóu jià.
皇帝的女儿不愁嫁。

The body of a princess but the fate of a slave girl
(champagne taste on a beer income; to have fancy tastes that far outstrip your means)

Xiǎojiě de shēnzi, yātou de mìng
小姐的身子，丫头的命

The barefoot person fears not those wearing shoes.
(People who are poor and powerless may feel they have nothing
to lose in standing up to the rich and powerful, if necessary.)
Guāng jiǎo de búpà chuān xié de.
光脚的不怕穿鞋的。

**If you're under the low-hanging eaves, how can you dare
not bow your head?**
(When you depend on others for food, lodging, or pay, you have
no choice but to bow to their wishes.)
Zài rén ǎi yán xià, zě gǎn bù dī tóu?
在人矮檐下，怎敢不低头？

**Three smelly cobblers combined equal a Zhuge Liang [an
Aristotle].**
(The combined wisdom of a number of ordinary people can
equal that of one genius, like the brilliant strategist of the third-
century BCE, Zhuge Liang; two heads are better than one.)
Sānge chòu píjiàng, còu ge Zhūgé Liàng.
三个臭皮匠，凑个诸葛亮。

**Generals and prime ministers were not born to greatness;
each man became so through great effort.**
Jiàng xiàng běn wú zhǒng, nán ér dāng zì qiáng.
将相本无种，男儿当自强。

If you're under the low-hanging eaves, how can you dare not bow your head?
在人矮檐下，怎敢不低头？

People need to ascend to a high place; water must flow ever downward.
(Said by parents to encourage their children to work to rise in life, rather than be like water that follows the natural law of gravity)
Rén wàng gāochù zǒu, shuǐ wàng dīchù liú.
人往高处走，水往低处流。

No one's ten fingers are all the same length.
(You cannot expect that everyone will be like you.)
Shíge zhǐtóu bù yìbān qí.
十个指头不一般齐。

Whoever has milk we regard as our mother.
(People will serve whoever makes it worth their while.)
Yǒu nǎi biàn shì niáng.
有奶便是娘。

Those involved do not grasp what the onlooker sees clearly.
(It's often easier for an outsider to see clearly what those involved in a troubled situation cannot.)
Dāng jú zhě mí, páng guān zhě qīng.
当局者迷，旁观者清。

Well borrowed and well returned makes it easy to borrow again.
(If when you borrow something you take care of it and return it promptly, you'll not find it difficult to borrow something again.)
Hǎo jiè hǎo huán, zài jiè bù nán.
好借好还，再借不难。

Even a wise person is sure to be mistaken one time out of a thousand; even a fool is sure to get something right one time out of a thousand.
(Even the smartest person isn't perfect, while even the dumbest person comes up with a good idea once in a blue moon.)
Zhìzhě qiān lǜ bì yǒu yìshī, yúzhě qiān lǜ bì yǒu yì dé.
智者千虑必有一失，愚者千虑必有一得。

The one who just stands around and criticizes [knows not] the aching back of those doing the work.
(Some people do, while others criticize; talk is cheap.)
Zhànzhe shuōhuà bù yāo téng.
站着说话不腰疼。

When you drink water, don't forget those who dug the well.
(Don't take for granted the hard work of those who came before you.)
Hē shuǐ búwàng jué jǐng rén.
喝水不忘掘井人。

喝水不忘掘井人

When you drink water, don't forget those who dug the well

One's ancestors planted the tree; their descendants enjoy the cool shade.

(We all owe a debt to those who came before us and left us so much.)

Qián rén zhòng shù, hòu rén chèng liáng.

前人种树，后人乘凉。

Distant water cannot quench present thirst.

(The promise of something to come is of no help when the need is immediate.)

Yuǎn shuǐ jiěbùliǎo jìn kě.

远水解不了近渴。

What you can do isn't hard; what's hard is what you can't do.

Huìzhě bùnán, nánzhě búhuì.

会者不难，难者不会。

Nothing in the world is difficult if one sets his mind to it.

(Where there's a will, there's a way; all that is required to accomplish anything is determination.)

Shìshàng wú nán shì, zhǐ pà yǒu xīn rén.

世上无难事，只怕有心人。

You can't judge people by their looks; you can't measure the ocean by the bushel.

(A person's true character is as difficult to fathom as the sea.)

Rén bù kě mào xiàng, hǎi shuǐ bù kě dǒuliáng.

人不可貌相，海水不可斗量。

A suspicious mind creates ghosts in the dark.

(A person always looking for problems sees them even when there are none.)

Yíxīn shēng àn guǐ.

疑心生暗鬼。

There is a different key for every lock.

(Different problems require different solutions.)

Yìbǎ yàoshí kāi yìbǎ suǒ.

一把钥匙开一把锁。

To untie the bell, you need the person who tied it.

(The person who created the problem should be the one to solve it.)

Jiě líng hái xū xì líng rén.

解铃还需系铃人。

To play the monk and strike the bell for a day

(to do one's work half-heartedly; the bell is the monk's call to worship)

Zuò yìtiān héshang zhuàng yìtiān zhōng

做一天和尚撞一天钟

When you save someone, save them all the way; when you see someone off, see them all the way home.

(Anything worth doing is worth doing right.)

Jiù rén jiù dào dǐ, sòng rén sòng dào jiā.
救人救到底，送人送到家。

Give a treasured sword to a brave warrior; give rouge to a beautiful woman.
(Gifts should suit the person to whom they're given.)
Bǎojiàn zèngyǔ lièshì, hóngfěn zèngyǔ jiārén.
宝剑赠与烈士，红粉赠与佳人。

To move a tree might kill it; to move people may give them (new) life.
(Moving to another place to live and work may give you a chance to start life anew.)
Rén nuó huó, shù nuó sǐ.
人挪活，树挪死。

As long as the green mountains exist, you'll never lack for firewood.
(Where there's life, there's hope.)
Liú dé qīng shān zài, bú pà méi chái shāo.
留得青山在，不怕没柴烧。

17 Proverbs That May Sound Familiar to English Speakers

Many Chinese sayings sound rather familiar to the English speakers, for two possible reasons. The first is that the Chinese have borrowed some expressions from English, such as "All roads lead to Rome" and "Necessity is the mother of invention." These sayings have been used so frequently for so long in China that the average Chinese person is not aware that they are borrowed from the West, any more than they realize that they are quoting one of Aesop's fables when they speak of "sour grapes." The second and most likely explanation is that "Great minds think alike" or, as the Chinese say, "Great heroes generally see things in the same way."

Up to this point, this book has featured countless examples of Chinese proverbs that express the same truths about our lives as do English-language proverbs, only in a slightly different way. Different cultures might use different metaphors to talk about the human experience but, ultimately, we are all one race, the human race. Our experience as human beings is very much the same across cultures. It is true, as Confucius said so long ago, that "all men are brothers"—we are all one family.

If you're too greedy, you'll chew more than you can swallow

贪多嚼不烂

[To kill] two birds with one stone
Yì shí liǎng niǎo
一石两鸟—*Aesop*

Every major road leads to Rome.
(All roads lead to Rome.)
Tiáo tiáo dà lù tōng Luómǎ.
条条大路通罗马。

Necessity is the mother of invention.
Xūyào shì fāmíng zhī mǔ.
需要是发明之母。

COMMON HUMANITY, COMMON WISDOM

Great heroes generally see things the same way.
(Great minds think alike.)
Yīngxióng suǒ jiàn lüè tóng .
英雄所见略同。

The son will inevitably be like his father.
(Like father, like son.)
Yǒu qí fù bì yǒu qí zǐ.
有其父必有其子。

Strike the iron [to form it] while it's hot.
(Strike while the iron's hot.)
Chèn rè dǎ tiě.
趁热打铁。

When you enter a country, follow its customs.
(When in Rome, do as the Romans do.)
Rù xiāng suí sú.
入乡随俗。

Eyes big, stomach small. (My eyes were bigger than my stomach.)
Yǎn dà dùzi xiǎo.
眼大肚子小。

If you're too greedy, you'll chew more than you can swallow.
(Don't bite off more than you can chew.)
Tān duō jiáobúlàn.
贪多嚼不烂。

[If you pay] one cent, [you get] one cent of merchandise.
(You get what you pay for.)
Yìfēn qián yìfēn huò.
一分钱一分货。

入乡随俗

When you enter a country, follow its customs

Expensive things aren't really expensive; cheap things aren't really cheap.
(Buy cheap, get cheap. See the same proverb in Chapter 6, above, in a different context.)
Guìde búguì, jiànde bújiàn.
贵的不贵，贱的不贱。

To destroy the bridge after crossing the river
(to pull up the ladder behind them; refers to selfish people who begrudge others from following their path to success by eliminating that path)
Guò hé chāi qiáo
过河拆桥

One [Buddhist] priest carries water to drink on a shoulder pole; two priests carry water to drink by each carrying one handle of the bucket; three priests have no water to drink.
(Many hands make light work, but too many cooks spoil the broth.)
Yīge héshang tiāo shuǐ chī; liǎngge héshang tái shuǐ chī; sānge héshang méi shuǐ chī.
一个和尚挑水吃；两个和尚抬水吃；三个和尚没水吃。

In the eyes of one in love, his beloved seems a Venus.
(actually "Xi Shi," a renowned beauty of ancient times; similar
to "Beauty is in the eye of the beholder")
Qíngrén yǎnlǐ chū Xī Shī.
情人眼里出西施。

One laugh can cure a hundred illnesses.
(Laughter is the best medicine.)
Yí xiào zhì yìbǎi bìng.
一笑治一百病。

18

Sayings Attributed to the Chinese—Rightly or Wrongly

After people in the West came to appreciate the great variety and profundity of Chinese proverbs, we began to collect them. Often the translations into English of the very pithy Chinese sayings were embellished to the point that it is difficult for someone who knows Chinese to recognize the source of the expression.

Many other sayings are falsely attributed to the Chinese. Although many English speakers firmly believe that the phrase "May you live in interesting times" is an ancient Chinese curse, no one has ever been able to discover its Chinese origin—but this is not important. What matters is that the proverb or saying offers some truth about life or is uplifting. The ones listed below are our personal favorites.

It is likely that most of these proverbs did not come from Chinese—for example, "A bird does not sing because it has an answer; it sings because it has a song." Many people in the English-speaking world are fond of it nonetheless.

Similarly, no Chinese person to our knowledge has discovered a Chinese source for the saying "Find a job you love and you'll never have to work a day in your life." But that does not stop us from repeating it to our students, as we encourage them to follow their passions in deciding on a future career. If, like us, they become teachers of Chinese and write books such as this, then they, too, will never have to work a day in their lives!

Fool me once, shame on you; fool me twice, shame on me.

Find a job you love, and you'll never have to work a day in your life.

A bird does not sing because it has an answer; it sings because it has a song.

A bit of fragrance clings to the hand that gives flowers.

A book is like a garden carried in one's pocket.

A child's life is like a sheet of paper on which every person leaves a mark.

When all you have left is two pennies, buy a loaf of bread with one and a lily with the other.

To learn the road ahead, ask those who are coming back.

A single spark can set a whole prairie on fire. (Perhaps inspired by a similar Chinese proverb, but so loosely translated as to be a newly minted English saying.)

One hand alone can't clap; it takes two to quarrel. (The Chinese proverb only includes the first half of this proverb, although it implies the second part.)

Happiness is not a horse; you cannot harness it.

Failure is not falling down but refusing to get up.

Index

A fast horse needs only one lash of the whip; a quick student needs only one word [of wisdom]. 15

A fat person didn't get fat with just one mouthful. 21, 131

A fox can never hide his tail. 120

A fox isn't aware its tail stinks. 121

After a word is spoken, even a team of four horses cannot catch up to it. 109

After something has passed through three mouths, even snakes are said to have grown legs. 35

After [too much] wine, there is no virtue. 48

A gentleman never argues with an ox. 111

A girl changes 18 times before becoming a woman. 87

A girl, once grown, cannot be kept at home. 87

A golden nest or a silver nest cannot compare to one's own humble [dog's] nest. 114

A good dog doesn't get under foot. 113

A good horse does not accept two saddles. 107

A good horse will never turn around to graze in an old pasture. 106

A great man is silent about his past glories. 26

A great person [has the courage to] accept the consequences of his own actions. 39

A haggard [starving] camel is still bigger than a horse. 110

A half-filled bottle makes noise [when shaken], while a full bottle makes none. 28

A horse doesn't know its face is long; an ox doesn't know its horns are crooked. 29

A hundred kinds of rice feed a hundred kinds of people. 133

A hundred people have a hundred different tastes [in food]. 133

A hundred years of age is like a traveler passing by. 66

A husband and wife are actually birds from the same woods, but when the end comes each flies away on its own. 84

A job for life; the livelihood you depend on 138

All crows the world over are black. 123

A long journey will prove the stamina of a horse; the passage of time will show a person's true heart. 107

Always remember in times of plenty the days when you had nothing; don't wait until you're poor again to recall fondly the times of plenty. 53

A mangy cur can't make it over a wall even when helped. 114

A man on horseback cannot understand how hard it is for a person who has to run [someone "under the horse"]; a sated man cannot understand how a hungry man feels. 108

A man who has no wife has no peace in his heart. 83

A monk may run away, but his temple can't run away. 47

A mouse can only see one inch in front of its nose. 120

A mouse will bravely shoulder a rifle in its own nest. 120

An amicable divorce is as important as an amicable marriage. 82

An ant who tries to topple a giant tree is laughable in his inability to know himself. 93

A newborn calf has no fear of tigers. 111

Anger between husband and wife should not last the night. 82

An old general who rides out on his horse [to battle] is worth any two others. 63

An old horse knows the way. 63, 110

An old person when healthy is like a chilly spring or a late autumn warm spell. 61

An opportunity can't be missed; if lost, it will never come again. 67

An ounce of gold can't buy an ounce of time. 65

An ugly (or inferior) man wanted to marry a young, pretty woman. 137

An ugly woman must still meet her in-laws. 88

An [unripe] melon torn from the vine isn't sweet. 133

A peony in bloom is a lovely thing, but it still needs the green leaves to support it. 58

A person may not intend to harm the tiger, but the tiger may be intent on harming you. 102

A person whose heart is not content is like a snake that tries to swallow an elephant. 118

A phoenix won't enter a crow's nest. 106

A poor man can stand by the roadside, but no one will ask how he is; a rich man can hide deep in the mountains, but distant relatives will come visit. 52

A poor man's ambition stops short; a thin horse's mane appears long. 52

A rabbit cannot be harnessed to [pull] a carriage. 116

A rabbit's tail can only grow so long. 116

A rabbit [when cornered] will turn around and become fierce as a tiger. 116

A room full of sons and daughter cannot equal (the value of) a husband and wife who share a mat (on which to sit). 82

Arrogance is the enemy of victory. 26

A sheep's wool must be taken off the sheep's body. 127

A single spark can set a whole prairie on fire. 159

A single thread cannot make a cord; a lone tree cannot make a forest. 57

As long as the green mountains exist, you'll never lack for firewood. 152

A snake cannot go anywhere when its head is gone; a bird cannot fly without its wings. 118

A son will always take after his father. 78

A sparrow may be tiny, but it has both a liver and a spleen [all internal organs]. 124

A spear openly thrust at you is easy to dodge; an arrow shot from hiding is hard to defend against. 40

A speedy horse doesn't need to be whipped to be urged on; a loud drum doesn't need to be struck with a heavy hammer. 107

A superior person knows what is moral; a petty person [only] knows what is profitable. 44

A suspicious mind creates ghosts in the dark. 151

A thankless task; to be a fool for one's pains 141

At home, rely on your parents; outside your door, rely on your friends. 73

A thousand friends are too few, but one enemy is too many. 72

A thousand-mile journey starts under your feet. 23

A tiger and a leopard each goes its own way. 102

A tiger father will not beget a puppy. 100

A tiger's head with a snake's tail 101

A tongue may weigh little, but it can crush a man. 34

At three years old, you can see the person when grown; at seven years old, you can see the person when old. 60

A victorious cat is like an overjoyed tiger. 122

A wise man does not argue with women. 88

A wolf will walk a thousand miles and still eat people; a dog will go to the end of the earth and still eat garbage. 113

Before you reach the age of 88, don't laugh at those who are lame or blind. 64

Better to be a bird's head than a cow's rump. 125

Better to be a broken piece of jade than an unbroken shard of clay tile. 45

Better to go without books than to believe everything they say. 18

[Beware of] a tiger with a smiling face. 103

Beyond the sky is another sky; beyond the mountain is another mountain. 27

Big fish can't be raised in a shallow pond. 126

Big fish eat little fish; small fish eat little shrimp. 125

Binding two people together does not make them husband and wife. 83

Birds without a head can't fly; wild beasts without a head can't walk. 125

Blessings never come in pairs, but misfortunes never come singly. 92

Camera for dummies, i.e., easy-to-use camera 137

Cats who love to meow can't catch mice. 121

Cheap things aren't good, and good things aren't cheap. 53

Cheese!, i.e., Smile! 136

Children and grandchildren will enjoy their own blessings [when grown]; there is no need to labor like a draft animal to ensure their futures. 80

Clearly knowing there are tigers on the mountain, yet still headed to the tiger mountain 101

Close your mouth and hide your tongue, and you can settle down safely
    anywhere. 33
Clothes make the man just as a saddle [with adornments] makes the horse. 109
Cold rice and cold soup are easy to eat, [but] cold words and cold speech are
    hard to bear. 36
Compare yourself to those who are superior to you, and you'll find yourself
    lacking; compare yourself to those who are inferior to you, and you'll find
    yourself more than good enough. 25

Dark clouds can't blot out the sun. 96
Dishes without salt are tasteless; words without reason are powerless. 36, 133
Distant water cannot quench present thirst. 150
Do not display to others your family's ugly problems. 77
Do not spend the whole day in idleness; your youth will never come again. 68
[Don't be like] a frog at the bottom of a well. 19
Don't cross the river before rolling up your trouser legs; don't open your mouth
    before knowing the true state of things. 32
Don't eat excessive amounts of food; don't indulge in excessive talk. 33
Don't fear a thousand-to-one chance that something bad might happen; fear the
    one chance in a thousand. 40
Don't fear going slow [making slow progress]; just fear standing still. 23
Don't let loose the falcon until you see the hare. 116
[Don't] pull on seedlings to help them grow. 23
Don't strike a dog until you see its master's face. 112
Dummy; silly guy 137

Each crab is smaller than the one before. 128
Each person should first clear away the snow from his own front door before
    worrying about the frost on his neighbor's roof. 39
Eat a full breakfast, eat a good lunch, but only eat a small supper. 135
Eat/suffer a fall into the pit, gain in your wit. 14
Enjoy together the happy times and face together times of trouble. 72
[Even] a clever woman cannot cook a meal without rice. 132
Even a family with a thousand people can only have one master. 77
Even a hero has trouble crossing the mountain pass of a beautiful woman. 84
Even a hundred-foot-high bamboo can still grow taller. 17
Even a skinny tiger has an ambitious heart. 103
Even a thousand miles apart, a couple destined for one another are pulled
    together by an [invisible] thread. 83
Even a tough man can't avoid [feeling] the wind by his pillow. 84
Even a wise person is sure to be mistaken one time out of a thousand; even a
    fool is sure to get something right one time out of a thousand. 149

Even if you've never eaten pork, surely, you've seen a pig run? 112

Even rabbits will bite you if desperate enough. 115

(Even) sumptuous feasts must end (eventually). 67

Even the most vicious tiger won't devour its cubs. 101

Even tigers sometimes doze/take a nap. 102

Even when there are no problems out there [in the world], foolish people create trouble for themselves. 95

Every family's classic saga has pages that are difficult to read. 77

Every major road leads to Rome. 154

Every master has his/her own teaching methods; every trick has a different sleight of hand. 12

Everything is controlled by fate and not in the slightest by people. 91

Everything is hard in the beginning. 23

Expensive things aren't really expensive; cheap things aren't really cheap. 54, 156

Eyes big, stomach small. (My eyes were bigger than my stomach.) 155

Failure is not falling down but refusing to get up. 160

Failure is the mother of success. 23

Familiarity can engender skill. 18

Fasten the gate after the sheep have already been lost. 128

Fear people who are of one mind [united by a common cause] as much as tigers gathered into a pack. 103

Fierce dogs bite people without showing their teeth. 115

Find a job you love, and you'll never have to work a day in your life. 159

First be a student, then be a teacher. 13

Follow a tiger, and you'll go into the mountains; follow an eagle, and you'll fly into the sky. 101

Food and clothing won't eat up your fortune, but lack of planning will. 131

Food must be eaten bite by bite; a road must be walked step by step. 21

Foolish people wag their tongues; wise people use their brains. 33

Fool me once, shame on you; fool me twice, shame on me. 159

From a crow's nest, a phoenix may emerge. 106

Gain a friend, and you gain one more path [away from worry]; lose an enemy, and you've lost one more obstacle [in your way]. 72

Generals and prime ministers were not born to greatness; each man became so through great effort. 147

Ginger gets spicier with age. 63

Give a man a fish, and he'll have food for a day [three meals]; teach a man to fish, and he'll have a skill to use all his life. 13

Give a treasured sword to a brave warrior; give rouge to a beautiful woman. 152

If it's not light in the east, then it's light in the west; if it's dark to the south, there's always the north. 96

If jade is not cut and polished, it can't be made into anything useful (and beautiful). 16

If man is iron, food is steel. 130

If previous experiences are not forgotten, they can be the teachers in later matters. 14

If the butcher lays down his knife, he has but to stand to become a Buddha [a saint]. 49

If the family lives in harmony, everything will go well for them. 77

If there's no wutong tree, you'll never attract a phoenix. 105

If the son is filial, his father's heart can rest easy. 80

If water is too clear [and pure], you can't raise fish. 71, 126

If you are fated for one another, you will meet though separated by a thousand miles; if you are not fated for one another, you will not encounter each other even when face to face. 83

If you are patient in one moment of anger, you can escape a hundred days of sorrow [and regret]. 39

If you compare yourself to others, it'll just get you angry. 25

If you do not experience anything, it's impossible to gain knowledge. 14

If you do nothing shameful during the day, there's no need to fear ghosts will come knocking at your door at night. 46

If you don't eat fish, your mouth won't smell fishy. 48

If you don't enter the tiger's den, how will you ever get the tiger's cubs? 99

If you don't have a long-range plan for the future, you'll find yourself with nothing in old age. 62

If you don't know someone, look carefully at his friends. 73

If you don't prune a tree, it won't become usable lumber; if you don't nurture a child, he won't become a true adult. 80

If you don't talk about my bald head, I won't laugh at your poor eyesight. 29

If you don't think three times before acting, you will have regret; if you restrain yourself in all things, you will have no worries. 39

If you don't want people to know [the wrong you did], then it's best not to do it. 47

If you don't work hard when you're young and strong, you'll lead a miserable life when old. 61

If you fail to plan far into the future, you'll soon have worries in the near term. 68

If you go easy on others, they'll go easy on you. 41

If you hang around vermilion pillars, you'll turn red; if you hang around ink, you'll turn black. 73

[If] you have accepted a meal from someone, your tongue is softened; if you accept gifts from someone, your arms' reach is shortened. 132

If you have good luck, there is no misfortune to fear; if you have bad luck, there's no way to escape it. 91

If you know [something], to recognize that you know it; and if you don't know [something], to realize that you don't know it—that is [true] knowledge. 19

[If you pay] one cent, [you get] one cent of merchandise. 53, 155

[If you] plant melons, [you] reap melons; [if you] plant beans, [you] reap beans. 45

If you're not members of the same family, you won't enter by that family's door. 78

If you're not willing to part with your child [temporarily, as bait], you'll never lure the wolf into your trap. 127

If you're too greedy, you'll chew more than you can swallow. 155

If you're under the low-hanging eaves, how can you dare not bow your head? 147

If your face is ugly, you can't blame the mirror. 27

If you sit and eat [all the time], even a mountain [of wealth] can be emptied. 131

If you study with a sorceress, you'll learn to dance about in a trance. 13

If you want people to know you, study diligently; if you are afraid for people to know you, don't do things that are wrong. 16

If you want to be a good person, seek good people as friends. 73

If you want [to do things] well, ask the old [for advice]. 63

If you wish to be the an extraordinary person, you have to taste the bitterest of the bitter. 131

In a large wood, you'll find every kind of bird. 125

Indigo comes from blue but exceeds blue [in its beauty]. 15

In front of short people, do not speak about shortness. 35

In the eyes of one in love, his beloved seems a Venus. 157

In the mountains, there are often trees a thousand years old, but there are few people in the world who are one hundred years old. 60

In the Yangtze River, the waves in back push forward the waves in front of them; each generation is even better than the previous one. 81

In this world if one has a friend who understands you, that friend seems near even in the farthest corners of the earth. 70

It doesn't matter whether a cat is white or black, as long as it can catch mice [it's a good cat]. 121

It is in the deepest mountains that tigers and leopards hide; it is in turbulent times that heroes emerge. 100

It is preferable to believe there's some truth to a rumor than to believe that there's nothing there. 34

It is preferable to tear down ten temples than to destroy one marriage. 83

It's common for people to add flowers to adorn [your] brocade [robe], but in snowy weather how many will send you charcoal [to heat your home]? 53

It's difficult to fathom what lies in people's hearts; it's hard to plumb the depths of the water in the ocean. 40

It's easier to obtain a thousand ounces of gold than to find one person who really understands you. 71

It takes one [full] year for a tree to start growing; it takes ten years for a person to start growing. 23

It takes three years to learn a horse's nature, but five years to know a person's heart. 109

Just when you have a leaky roof, you'll meet with a prolonged rain storm; just when your boat needs repairs, you'll meet with a head wind. 92

Kill a chicken to frighten the monkeys. 117

Kill the hen to get the eggs. 117

Kind words need not be spoken behind people's backs; words spoken behind people's backs are rarely kind. 34

Learning has no boundaries. 18

Learning is like rowing a boat against the current; if you don't advance, you'll regress. 18

Learning without thinking is ignorance; thinking without learning (study) is dangerous. 19

Letting your illness go untreated is [as dangerous as] raising a tiger. 103

Like a mouse who encounters a cat 119

Like a praying mantis trying to block a chariot with its little arms 93

Like blind men touching an elephant [from the Buddhist scriptures] 128

Like two grasshoppers tied by the same thread 128

Listening to the [good] advice of others, you will enjoy many hearty meals. 37

Live 'til you're old and study 'til you're old, but there's still 30% you'll never learn. 17

Looking from this mountain, that yonder mountain seems higher. 26

Many little drops of water can turn into a [mighty] river. 22

Men should fear entering the wrong profession; women should fear marrying the wrong man. 88

Money allows you to speak with the gods. 51

Money resolves all matters just as a fire roasts a pig's head. 51

Necessity is the mother of invention. 154

Neither eat things haphazardly nor gossip haphazardly. 133

Never harm another, but beware of others who may intend to harm you. 40

Never hit a man in the face; never curse a man for his weaknesses. 35

Never pull on your shoes in a melon patch; never adjust your cap under a plum tree. 38

Never tire of studying, and never tire of teaching others. 12

Never use your influence completely; never show off your wealth completely; never take advantage completely; never display your cleverness completely. 41

No flower stays red for a hundred days. 67

No fly will latch onto uncracked eggs. 128

No ivory can come out of a dog's mouth. 113

No matter how big your hands may be, they can't cover the whole sky. 47

No one's ten fingers are all the same length. 148

No talk and no laughter is no way to live. 38

Nothing in the world is difficult if one sets his mind to it. 150

Of the myriad sins, lewdness heads the list; of the many virtues, filial piety is the first. 81

Old Wang praises his own melons while he sells them. 28

Once a word is spoken, even a team of four horses cannot catch up to it. 37

Once bitten by a snake in the morning, a person will fear the rope at the well for the next three years. 118

One [Buddhist] priest carries water to drink on a shoulder pole; two priests carry water to drink by each carrying one handle of the bucket; three priests have no water to drink. 156

One can know the world without going outside. One can see the Way of Heaven without looking out the window. 19

One day of not seeing [a dear one seems] like three autumns. 66

One day together as husband and wife is like a hundred days of grace. 81

One false step can cause life-long regret. 45

One grain of mouse droppings will ruin an entire pot of soup. 120

One hand alone can't clap; it takes two to quarrel. 160

One laugh can cure a hundred illnesses. 157

One mudfish can't stir up big waves. 126

One raises children to provide against old age, just as one stores grain to provide against famine. 78

One's ancestors planted the tree; their descendants enjoy the cool shade. 150

One who is burning with impatience can never eat hot porridge. 21

One who is starving is not picky about food. 134

Only if you have endured the bitterest suffering can you become a superior person. 15

[Only] one radish per hole 145

Only when the water in the big river is high will the small streams rise. 57

Only when the wok is full can [people's] bowls be filled. 57

Other people's wives always seem better than your own; [but] your own children always seem better than other people's. 79

Out of hunger comes wisdom; out of poverty comes cleverness. 15

People die in pursuit of wealth; birds die in pursuit of food. 52, 124

People die like an [oil] lamp going out. 61

People fear being poor in old age; rice fears a cold wind in late autumn. 64

People fear getting famous; pigs fear getting fat. 57, 111

People fear their minds [and spirits] getting old, as trees fear their roots becoming old. 64

People have a face [just as] a tree has bark. 35

People live only one lifetime, just as grass grows for only one autumn. 61

People may have a slip of the hand; horses may lose their footing. 107

People need to ascend to a high place; water must flow ever downward. 148

People will eat/accept softness when they'll refuse to eat/accept hardness. 132

Purposely plant flowers, and the flowers won't necessarily blossom; mindlessly stick a willow sapling in the ground, and it may grow to give you shade. 94

Rabbits never eat the grass that borders their burrow. 115

Real gold does not fear the furnace. 45

Receive one blow, and you'll learn a lesson; receive ten blows, and you'll end up a genius. 15

Requiring a lot of effort; strenuous 140

Saving a life is better than building a seven-story pagoda. 44

Sickness enters through the mouth; misfortune comes out of it. 31

Sour grapes 136

Spare the rat to save the dish. 120

Speaking well is not as good as acting well. 37

Strike the iron [to form it] while it's hot. 155

Sweet words and pretty talk keep people warm for the three months of winter; cruel speech wounds people and leaves them cold for six months. 36

Teachers open the door; you enter by yourself. 16

Teaching by example is better than teaching by preaching. 13

That's a shame; that's too bad 136

The barefoot person fears not those wearing shoes. 147

The bird that sticks its head out is the first to get shot. 56

The body of a princess but the fate of a slave girl 146

The dragon who swims in shallow water becomes the sport of shrimp; the tiger who descends to level ground may be bullied by dogs. 104

The emperor's daughter need not worry about [a lack of] suitors. 146

The fool does not ask; he who asks is no fool. 27

The foolish old man moved the mountain. 22

The friendship between two superior people is clear as shallow water; interaction between petty people is sweet as honey. 71

The heavens will rain, and women will want to marry. 92

The highest form of doing good is like water; water benefits all things but does seek anything (for itself). 43

The husband of a virtuous wife seldom suffers misfortune. 82

[The lack of] one penny can worry to death even the bravest of heroes. 54

The mightiest dragon can't overcome the chief snake of the district. 118

The moon waxes only to wane; water fills to the brim only to overflow. 28

The mouth and tongue have always been the roots of calamity. 31

The mouth is the door to disaster; the tongue is the knife that can kill you. 32

The old man on the border loses a horse; who knows if it isn't good fortune [in disguise]? 93

The one who just stands around and criticizes [knows not] the aching back of those doing the work. 149

The palm and the back of your hand are both your own flesh. 79

The people are the foundation of the country, and food is of the highest importance to the people. 130

The rafter that sticks out is the first to rot. 57

The raw rice has already been cooked. 134

There are three types of unfilial behavior, the greatest of which is to have no descendants. 81

There is a different key for every lock. 151

There is no banquet that doesn't eventually break up. 135

There is no end of books to read, [just as there is] no end of roads to travel. 17

There is strength in numbers; more firewood makes a bigger fire. 58

The sea of suffering is boundless, [but] if you turn around you'll spy the shore. 49

The seasons yield to no one. 67

The son will inevitably be like his father. 155

The springtime of one's life passes quickly, and white hair is hard to avoid. 61

The tigers of East Mountain are man-eaters, as are the tigers of West Mountain. 100

The tip of the tongue, though soft, can sting people. 35

The tongue is the source of both benefits and harm; the mouth is a door that opens to either disaster or blessings. 31

The truth is not always present in the loudest voice. 37

The whole year's plan depends on a good start in spring; the whole day's work depends on a good start at dawn. 68

The wily hare has three holes to his burrow. 115

The wind may arise and the clouds appear in the sky without warning; people's fortunes may change between dawn and dusk of the same day. 91

Things don't go as we'd like 80–90% of the time. 92

Those involved do not grasp what the onlooker sees clearly. 148

Those who know that they have enough are always happy. 26

Those who retreated 50 paces [running away in battle] laugh at those who retreated 100 paces. 29

Three smelly cobblers combined equal a Zhuge Liang [an Aristotle]. 147

Three women [together] make for a lively comedy (lit. folk opera). 87

To accept an invitation to dinner [usually in return for a favor granted] 142

To add feet when painting a snake 119

To add pupils to the eyes of the dragon you're painting 105

To be cheated but unable to speak out about it 143

To be denied entrance at the door; to be refused admission as an unwelcome guest 139

To be forced to suffer in silence 144

To be hard-pressed; to be in a critical situation 140

To be in a bad mood and not amenable to reason; irritable 141

To be insatiably greedy; never satisfied 144

To be in the king's company is tantamount to being in the company of a tiger. 99

To be looked on with contempt; be looked down upon 139

To be paid in spite of not making much of an effort 141

To be shot dead by a bullet 141

To be sued in a court of law 140

To be surprised/alarmed 136

To be suspicious; overly sensitive 143

To be treated in a favored way; to enjoy some kind of privilege 143

To be very popular; to be much sought after 142

To be yelled at and beaten like a rat who runs across the street 119

To catch a big fish, one must cast a long line. 125

To catch fish to eat, first grab a hold of the head. 126

To cry over spilled milk 140

To destroy the bridge after crossing the river 156

To do something senselessly 138

To eat a chestnut, you have to remove the shell; to lead an ox, you have to lead it by the nose. 110

To eat fish but complain of the fishy taste 131

To eke out a living as a lowly paid teacher 139

Trees, when old, have more roots; people, when old, have more life experience. 62

Two bitter melons on the same vine 145

Two tigers can't remain on the same mountain together. 102

Until the cooking is done, don't lift the lid off the wok. 134

Walk often by the river's edge, and your shoes are bound to get wet. 48

Well borrowed and well returned makes it easy to borrow again. 149

We only sleep best right before dawn; people learn wisdom only in old age. 62

What you can do isn't hard; what's hard is what you can't do. 150

What you do not want done to you, do not do to other people. 44

What you learn depends on whom you study with; if you study with a butcher, you'll never become a cobbler. 13

When all you have left is two pennies, buy a loaf of bread with one and a lily with the other. 159

When a man is kind, people will cheat him; when a horse is gentle, people will ride him. 108

When a man is poor, his ambition does not reach far; when a horse is skinny, its hair appears long. 108

When a man passes away, all he leaves behind is his reputation; when a wild goose passes by, all he leaves is his cry. 123

When a person is desperate, he'll rebel and fight back; when a dog is desperate, it'll even leap over a wall. 114

When a weasel comes to pay his respects to the chicken at the new year, he harbors no good intentions. 121

When drinking with a kindred spirit, a thousand cups of wine seem too few; when conversing with an incompatible person, half a sentence seems too much. 72

When eating, take care not to choke; when walking, take care you don't fall. 134

When horses get old, no one rides them; when people get old, they are taken for a ride. 63

When in a stable to buy a horse, take a good look at its mother. 78, 109

When meeting people, say only 30% [of what you're thinking]; don't toss out everything that's in your mind. 33

When one dog barks at a shadow, a hundred bark at the sound. 115

When people are of one mind, they can fill in the oceans and move mountains. 58

When people grow old or pearls become yellow [with age], there is no medicine to cure them. 64

When people turn 50 [years old], they're like tigers descending the mountain. 104

When seeing off a dear friend, there must finally be a farewell. 67

When seeing off close friends and relations, the road seems [too] short; when returning to one's home, the road seems [too] long. 66

When shooting at a man, first shoot his horse; when catching robbers, first catch their leader. 109

When striking/attacking a snake, first strike its head. 117

When the horse is slow, we complain that the whip is used too lightly; when we're impatient, we complain that the cart is too slow. 110

When there's no food in the trough, pigs will jostle one another. 111

When there's no wine [left] in the pot, it's hard to get your guests to stay. 53

When the snipe and the clam fight, it's the fisherman who profits. 124

When the tree falls, the monkeys will scatter. 127

When trees are big [tall], they invite the wind [to knock them down]. 56

When trees get old, their trunks become half-empty [hollow]; when people get old, they are full of knowledge about many things. 17

When two tigers tussle, one is bound to get injured. 102

When we walk together with three people, (at least) one of them will have something to teach us. 12

When you can't even put yourself to rights, how can you hope to transform others? 29

When you drink water, don't forget those who dug the well. 149

When you enter a country, follow its customs. 155

When your belly is empty, you can't wait for the early rice to turn yellow [ripen]. 134

When your cart comes to a mountain, there's always a way [around it]. 95

When you're enjoying yourself, you complain the night is too short; when you are lonely, you lament that each hour is so long. 66

When your hair is in disarray, look for a comb; when your heart is in disarray, look for a friend. 70

When you save someone, save them all the way; when you see someone off, see them all the way home. 151

When you should let others off the hook, you must let them off the hook; when you should pardon others, you had best pardon them. 41

Where is there a cat who won't steal fish? OR Where is there a rat who won't steal oil? 122

Where the mountains end and the rivers peter out and you despair of ever finding the way, there beyond the dark willows and bright flowers lies another village. 94

Whoever has milk we regard as our mother. 148

Whoever is your teacher, even for a day, consider your father (to respect and care for) your whole life. 12

Who is never gossiped about behind his back, and who never gossips about
   people to others? 34
Why use a knife designed to butcher cattle to kill a chicken? 116
Wielding the ax in front of Ban's gate 28
Wild geese fear being separated from the flock; people fear falling behind the
   group. 123
With enough work, an iron rod can be ground into a needle. 22
"Within the four seas, all men are brothers." 10
With money, you can even get the devil to push the millstone for you. 51
Without experiencing the cold of winter, one cannot appreciate the warmth of
   spring. 14
Women can hold up half the sky. 88
Women may be long on hair, but they're short on knowledge. 88

You are never too old to learn. 17
You can hold other people's hands [down], but you can't get them to hold their
   tongues. 34
You can't conceal fire by wrapping it in paper. 47
You can't judge people by their looks; you can't measure the ocean by the
   bushel. 151
You can't tell whether or not a stuffed bun has meat inside just from looking at
   the outside. 132
You have to run your own household to know the price of rice and firewood;
   you have to raise your own children to understand the sacrifices that
   parents make. 80
You may be able to draw [sketch] a tiger's skin, but it's much harder to draw its
   bones; you may know a person's face, but it's difficult to know his heart. 100
You only get criticized if you open your mouth too much; troubles all come from
   trying to show off. 32
You try to draw a tiger but end up only drawing a dog. 101
You want your horse to run while not wanting it to eat grass [get
   nourishment]. 108

OTHER TITLES BY QIN XUE HERZBERG AND LARRY HERZBERG

China Survival Guide
How To Avoid Travel Troubles and Mortifying Mishaps, Revised Edition

This entertaining and informative guide to China offers insider's perspectives on how to maneuver through common travel and cultural issues. Learn the secrets to Chinese bathrooms, hotels, airports, hospitals, haggling, eating, shopping, medical, etiquette, plus practical planning and cultural observations. Includes useful Chinese phrases, and resource lists.

232 pp, 4½ x 6", paper, 60 b/w photos, ISBN 978-1-933330-94-5, $9.95.

Basic Patterns of Chinese Grammar
A Student's Guide to Correct Structures and Common Errors

Here is a concise guide to supplement any course of study and help with homework, travel, and test preparation. Topics include word order, time, nouns, verbs, adjectives, word choices with verbs and adverbs, and letter writing. The simple format has one goal: quick mastery and growing confidence.

128 pp, 5½ x 8½" paper, ISBN 978-1-933330-89-1, $12.95.

Available at booksellers worldwide and online.